TH
POWER
OF
CRYSTALS

Practices to Enhance Health,
Harmony, and Happiness

JULIET MADISON

ixia
PRESS

Mineola, New York

Bibliographical Note

The Power of Crystals: Practices to Enhance Health, Harmony, and Happiness
is a new work, first published by Ixia Press in 2020.

Library of Congress Cataloging-in-Publication Data

Names: Madison, Juliet, author.
Title: The power of crystals : practices to enhance health, harmony, and happiness / Juliet Madison.
Description: Mineola : Ixia Press, 2020. | Includes bibliographical references and index. | Summary: "Discover the secrets behind the power of crystals to enhance the connections between mind, body, and spirit. This beautifully illustrated guide explains the nature of crystals and how they work: their role in meditation, intention-setting, and manifesting; creating displays and altars; wearing them as jewelry; their employment in vision boards; and much more. Specific uses for cultivating health, family harmony, and career success are also explored. Juliet Madison is a best-selling and award-nominated author of nineteen books, including the inspirational adult coloring book *Color Your Dreams* and the self-help journal *The Secret Letters Project*. She is a writing coach and a life coach who creates and facilitates online courses for those seeking self-empowerment for mind, body, and spirit. Juliet has also practiced as a naturopath and is a certified facilitator of the Passion Test. She lives in Australia"— Provided by publisher.
Identifiers: LCCN 2019022565 | ISBN 9780486835464 (trade paperback)
Subjects: LCSH: Crystals—Miscellanea.
Classification: LCC BF1442.C78 M33 2020 | DDC 133/.2548—dc23
LC record available at https://lccn.loc.gov/2019022565

Ixia Press
An imprint of Dover Publications, Inc.

Manufactured in the United States by LSC Communications
83546401
www.doverpublications.com/ixiapress

2 4 6 8 10 9 7 5 3 1
2019

CONTENTS

Introduction   1

Chapter 1: Physical Health   29

Chapter 2: Emotional Well-being   41

Chapter 3: Self-love   53

Chapter 4: Healthy Relationships   63

Chapter 5: Attracting Love   74

Chapter 6: Family Harmony   87

Chapter 7: Creating a Safe Home Sanctuary   97

Chapter 8: Workplace Harmony, Career Dreams,
            and Lifelong Learning   110

Chapter 9: Fertility and Pregnancy   127

Chapter 10: Financial Abundance   145

Chapter 11: Sleep and Dreams   157

Chapter 12: Chakra Balancing and Energy Healing   169

Chapter 13: Children and Crystals   184

Chapter 14: Confidence and Communication   195

Chapter 15: Spiritual and Intuitive Development   211

            Acknowledgments   231

            Index of Crystals   233

            About the Author   235

INTRODUCTION

How I Discovered the Power of Crystals

I think people are drawn to crystals when the time is right for them. For me, it was when I was looking for a gift for someone special, who is a nature lover and who was being affected by a negative situation at the time. But I had no idea which crystals to choose or where to buy them. With my background in natural health and interest in all things spiritual and with friends and colleagues who often spoke of crystals, it actually took me quite a while to get into them.

I found a store that recommended a chunk of black tourmaline. It didn't look that pretty, but it was supposed to protect against negative influences. The gift was well received, and I began going regularly to New Age stores, discovering new crystals and their power. My collection gradually grew and so did my interest and knowledge. I created little displays in my house and began holding crystals as I meditated. I also visited the breathtaking Crystal Castle in Byron Bay, Australia, home of the world's largest crystals. I could literally feel the positive energy there becoming part of me and enhancing what was already part of me. I felt a strong connection to the crystals and to the spirit of Mother Nature, as though my intuitive and manifesting power had increased simply by being surrounded by all the crystal energy. Within minutes after we left, an expensive item my partner had been trying to sell for months on eBay suddenly sold. It was as though all resistance had been released and everything started aligning back to a state of peace, love, and abundance.

Since that day when I was looking for a gift, it seemed like crystals were becoming a guide for me, steering me in the right direction in my career and personal life. New opportunities came up that were more in sync with who I was. Old habits and connections that I no longer resonated with slipped away, and new ways and new connections appeared, as though my life was gathering momentum in the direction I was meant to go.

As an artist from a young age, I started feeling the urge to paint again. Crystals found their way into my artworks, and I glued small pieces on to my paintings. I found a local store to rent some table space from where I could sell my art, but I needed something more to sell to make it worthwhile. "Why don't you also sell crystals?" the store manager asked. It was a light bulb moment for me. *Could I? Instead of visiting crystal stores as a customer, could I really create my own little store?* Within a couple of weeks, I found a supplier and was set up. I was so excited, displaying all my new babies on the shelves, even though I would not be keeping them for myself. I loved knowing that I could provide something special for someone who came in looking for a gift or the perfect crystal for themselves. My little crystal table then became a space within a larger store of local handmade items and gifts, and along with my partner, I began running crystal activity workshops for kids.

One day while meditating, I had a vision appear in my mind. I already had been doing intuitive readings for people via e-mail, but I hadn't incorporated crystals before. In the vision, I saw myself holding a crystal and handing it to someone, along with a message I had received for them. Around the same time, I received an opportunity to do some face-to-face readings at a local outdoor market, and so I decided that I would start incorporating crystals as I had seen in my vision. And then began my experience of crystal communication, the crystals acting as a kind of conduit or focal point of energy for receiving insights from the spiritual realm. Clients would choose a crystal, think about their life and their questions, and then I would hold the crystal and give them a crystal "reading." I still work this way for most readings, even for distance readings (the only difference being that I choose the crystal to work with). Crystals have become my entourage of little helpers.

While I was enjoying my newfound hobby and business, yet another opportunity came my way: my literary agent contacted me to ask if I would be interested in writing a book. It had crossed my mind briefly at one point, but I didn't think I had the time, so I dismissed it almost as quickly as I thought about it. But one of my beliefs is if a good opportunity presents itself to you, it does so for a reason and it would not be given to you if you could not do it, so it is therefore worth pursuing. I said yes and came up with a concept and proposal, and this book is the result.

I always have been a go-getter, working hard behind the scenes and striving for my goals and dreams, but I never "looked" for any of these opportunities. They came to me naturally, organically, and in perfect timing. And that is one of the wonderful ways in which crystal energy works: it draws to it and to you the things, people, and experiences that match its vibration or that resonate with its purpose.

I believe that each crystal is a representation of an aspect of ourselves, empowering us to embrace and embody that aspect with the help of its powerful energy and strengthening the link between our physical, emotional, and spiritual selves so that we can live fuller expressions of who we really are. By helping you tune in to your own needs and your true self, crystals have the power to help bring about positive changes and opportunities in your life, making it a more magical, miraculous, and meaningful journey.

How to Use This Book

In this introduction, you will find information about crystals and how they work, as well as ways you can use them. And in the following chapters you will discover how to benefit from specific crystals in all areas of your life. The chapters are divided into different life areas or purposes, so you can read them in any order you wish or turn to the topic you most want to work with first and find out which crystals will be most helpful. You also will find different tips and activities to integrate crystals into your life, and complementary tools and techniques to give you an overall approach to enhancing those aspects of your life. Some crystals are mentioned and described in more than one chapter, so there may be overlap between topics. Each crystal description and affirmation is tailored so that you can learn how that crystal relates to the particular topic.

How Crystals Are Formed and Where They Come From

Crystals are natural parts of our earth, often taking millions of years to be created. They are part of our history, stored within rocklike specimens. Crystals are formed from a combination of natural materials, elements, minerals, and gases under intense heat and pressure, liquefying or creating bubbles, solidifying and forming a variety of different crystalline structures and layers, and producing various patterns, shapes, and colors that depend on the particular constituents present and the amount of heat and pressure and time taken to solidify. They are Mother Nature's works of art.

Some crystals are found only in certain geographical locations, while others are more widespread in many parts of the world. The rarer the crystal or harder to obtain, the higher the cost.

The Secret behind the Power of Crystals and How They Work

Due to the intensity behind a crystal's creation and the amount of time taken to form, crystals hold a huge amount of energy and information from the earth. And with their highly concentrated nature and high vibrations of the atoms within, crystals are focused sources and transmitters of positive energy as well as absorbers of energy. For example, quartz crystals form the basis for much of our technology, from LCD screens to watches, because they can absorb and transmit energy. Different crystals vibrate at various frequencies, and these frequencies will resonate with different properties. For years, healers from around the world have known of the power of crystals and developed knowledge about the benefits of them, passing this on over time to future generations. In addition, because the earth is always evolving (as are we), crystals are evolving too, bringing with their evolution new information and properties that go beyond what they may be originally known for. So learning about crystals is never black and white; it is a field of study that is expanding as we gain more experience with how these natural gifts can help improve our lives.

All matter, including a crystal, is energy: atoms vibrating at different speeds and different frequencies or patterns, creating unique resonances with different effects. But energy is not just chemical, it is also spiritual. And so these gems contain the same life force that powers our own creation and life, and thus we are always connected to crystals and their energy, both by our physical similarities in terms of nature's elements and by our spiritual source that is the basis for all things.

Shapes and Forms

The crystals that you buy in stores are available in several different forms and shapes, including raw specimens or clusters, geodes, tumbled stones, pyramids, points, hearts, slices, cubes, spheres, wands, animal shapes, and even massage rollers.

Raw specimens are like chunks of rock, have rough edges, and may be duller in appearance. Clusters contain many little points and facets and sometimes look like tiny cities with towers sprouting from a base.

Geodes are like mini caves, with an outer rock wall and crystal interior and a hollowed-out area in the middle. Common geodes are agate, amethyst, and citrine.

Tumbled stones are often the most popular forms of crystals to buy, due to their usually inexpensive cost and ease of carrying around or using in daily life, as well as their beautiful surface and brighter colors from the rough edges being smoothed and polished.

Pyramids are crystals that have been fashioned into a sharp pyramid shape and are known for being great amplifiers of energy because the crystal energy converges into the sharp point at the top. They can be used in the center of a crystal grid (see pages 21–22) to enhance intentions and manifestations.

Points are also powerful crystals with a convergence point at the top, but are longer and taller and have a "tower" appearance with a few flattened surfaces. For example, some are formed as a hexagonal shape that converges into the middle at the top, focusing energy and pointing it upward. They also can be called "generators." Some crystals can have a single point at the top with a flat base or may have a point at both ends.

Heart-shaped crystals are popular for decorating and symbolizing love and also for working with the healing energy of love more directly. Rose quartz is particularly popular, as it is known as the "love crystal."

Slices of crystals are available, usually from agate crystals, due to their layers that create beautiful line patterns of varying color intensities. These are often made into jewelry and are great for laying flat against the skin, which enables them to work directly with the body.

Cubes are like crystal blocks. Some are formed into cubic structures naturally, but you will often find crystals shaped into perfectly symmetrical cubes in stores, and these are great for stabilizing energy and feeling grounded in yourself and your environment.

Spheres are the crystal balls of the crystal world. They radiate crystal energy all around and are good for holding in your hands while meditating or displaying on a stand in a room to spread high-vibration energy to all areas. Therefore, they can help with balancing the energy in a room.

Crystal wands may be cylindrical or have a tapered end, allowing the user to hold the wand while directing more focused energy to a specific area.

Some crystals are made into animal shapes, such as elephants and frogs, either for children or to represent different things such as good luck and prosperity. They are a great way to get youngsters into the healing power of crystals.

Crystal massage rollers or face rollers are very popular. They have a slightly curved cylindrical shape attached to a roller, making it glide smoothly against the skin. Some have a small roller on one end and a larger roller on the other end, and they are often used in facials or skin treatments to boost circulation, enhance the lymphatic system, and relieve fluid retention and puffiness. The benefit of the massage action is combined with the properties of the particular crystal, allowing the healing vibrations to be focused into the skin.

When choosing a crystal to use for something in particular, consider which shape is best for the purpose you are intending.

How to Choose the Right Crystals

There are several ways you can choose the crystals that are right for you. You can research crystal properties and purposes and obtain those that suit your needs, you can choose crystals based on the colors you like and those that you find visually appealing, or you can let your intuition guide you to the crystals that feel right. You also can pick crystals for each of your chakras (see pages 173–180) or your star sign or birth month.

When selecting based on properties and purpose, use the topics in this book to guide you. Decide which areas of your life are most important to you right now, and follow some of the crystal recommendations and activities for that topic. When there are several to choose from, you can use your own guidance and intuition to refine your choices to the most appropriate crystals.

A fun way to select some crystals to work with is to simply go to a store and pick up those that you like the look of and then check what their meanings are. You might find they actually suit your needs. You can do the same by allowing your intuition to tell you which crystals are right for you, which may or may not be those you find visually attractive. Let your hand roam above the crystals and naturally pick up any that you feel drawn to. You may wish to hold one at a time for a few moments to see if you can feel anything and make a short list of options before choosing the ones that you need right now.

If you are new to crystals, you may like to start off with a few basics. Here are examples of a good starter kit:

- amethyst (spiritual connection)
- rose quartz (love and peace)

- black tourmaline (protection)
- selenite (cleansing and calming)
- citrine (abundance and happiness)
- quartz (all-around energy enhancer)

Preparing and Cleansing Your Crystals

When you first bring a new crystal home, it is a good idea to cleanse it before displaying or using it. This is because crystals absorb energy easily, and although they are naturally protective and give off good energy, sometimes they can hold residual energy from previous use or contact with other people. Some crystals, such as carnelian and kyanite, are natural cleansers in their own right and do not tend to retain negative energy. Many crystal users feel they do not necessarily need cleansing, but it does not hurt to put those ones with your other crystals when cleansing . . . just in case. You also can use a stone such as carnelian to cleanse your other crystals, combined with the intention of that being its purpose.

Two of the best ways to cleanse are by placing the crystals outdoors, under the light of the sun for a few hours and/or under a full moon overnight. If you have to wait a while for the next full moon, you can still leave them out in moonlight, but you may need to do it for a few nights in a row to get a stronger cleansing effect.

Some crystals can be cleansed with fresh water, salt water, or seawater. Simply place the crystals in a small hessian bag or another porous material bag, let the water run over them, and then allow them to air dry.

You also can burn sage around your crystals or use an energy-cleansing spray to remove residual energy buildup or cleanse with a strong and genuine intention stated out loud, asking for all negative or old energy that does not serve you to be removed.

Soil can have a cleansing effect on your crystals too. You can bury them in rich, healthy soil and leave them for a while (just remember they are there!), or immerse them in the soil with your hands and state your intention.

In addition, music and sound can have healing and cleansing effects and work quickly, especially sound bowls or singing bowls, which you can get from many crystal or New Age stores. Simply place the crystals next to the sound bowl, but not touching it, and using the accompanying mallet, gently tap the side of the bowl and glide the mallet around the rim of the bowl, sustaining and radiating the sound vibration.

Once your crystals are cleansed, you may enjoy them for display or basic use, or you may program them with your intention for their purpose. If you do not have a specific purpose and just like having them around, you can simply hold them in your hands or hold your hands over them and say, "I ask that these crystals embody high vibrations of love and positivity and serve the highest good of myself and others." You can reword this intention to make it more specific to the purposes you wish to use them for, such as love, health, abundance, harmony, energy, and concentration. For example, if programming a crystal to help with finances, you could say, "I ask that this crystal hold the highest vibrations of abundance and serve my highest good in attracting joyful abundance into my life." You also can be more specific with your intentions. For example, "I ask that this crystal hold the highest vibrations of abundance and assist me in finding the perfect new job opportunity."

Crystals are wonderful focal points for directing your intentions and, when combined with conscious intent, help to enhance manifesting power.

Cautions

Some crystals, like selenite, can dissolve in water, and others may become weakened or fragile, such as kyanite, which is friable, so make sure to keep them indoors and away from moisture. Some crystals, such as malachite, can be toxic in their raw form, so make sure you only obtain polished forms and do not use them in crystal water elixirs. When in doubt, don't! Cleanse most crystals in sunlight or moonlight, and use in dry areas. It also goes without saying to be cautious with crystals around babies and young children, who love to put things into their mouths. Though the presence of crystals can be beneficial for them due to their healing and calming energies, small stones can be risky if they look like sweets or candy. So make sure you use larger-sized crystals in children's rooms and keep them up on a high shelf, or use smaller stones for specific purposes with your supervision and then put them away in a safe place afterward.

How You Can Use Crystals

Now for the fun part! After your crystals are cleansed and prepared, you can decide how you are going to use them. There are numerous ways to use crystals.

Some are obvious, like displaying them around your home, and some are not so obvious, such as creating crystal grids for setting intentions. Listed below are a variety of ways to make use of crystals, and then in the following chapters you will discover how these and other strategies can be integrated in different ways to assist with a particular area of your life.

MEDITATION

The benefits of regular meditation are well-documented, and when you meditate with crystals, the benefits can be enhanced, even more so when combined with intentions or visualizations. The purpose of meditation is to quiet and calm the mind and relax the body, helping with overall mental and physical well-being as well as assisting with depression and anxiety. You can use crystals during your meditation practice to help even further by simply holding a crystal or two in your hands, placing them on your body or under a pillow, or just having them nearby. Before meditating, set your intention for your crystal and how you would like it to help. You may simply ask it to help you relax and deepen your meditation session, or you may wish for it to have a more specific purpose, such as bringing you insight or answers from your intuition or from spirit or helping a health condition to improve. To start trying the effects of meditating with crystals, use an amethyst first, which is great for calming and tuning in to your inner guidance.

GOALS, INTENTIONS, AND MANIFESTING

Crystals can be used when needed for assisting with your goals and intention setting. They can be a powerful manifesting tool and a visual reminder for you about your goals. Which crystal you use depends on your specific goal, so use one for the particular purpose you are intending or one that you feel strongly drawn to.

When setting goals or intentions, you can use a crystal such as quartz or fluorite first to help you with clarifying what your goals and intentions are and then have an appropriate crystal to hold when stating your intentions out loud. You also can keep a list of your goals written down somewhere you will see them regularly and place a crystal on top of the paper so that the crystal embodies the energy of the goals and transmits its positive energy to them.

When writing down intentions and affirmations or using other positive journaling techniques, try holding your crystal in one hand as you write with the other, placing your chosen crystal next to you as you write, or attaching a small crystal to the top of your pen.

You can make use of the healing and supportive energy of the moon by creating a new moon intention ritual. After writing down your intentions, state them out loud while outdoors under the moon and program your crystals with these intentions by holding them as you read the intentions. The new moon is a time that symbolizes beginnings and fresh energy coming through to assist you with your goals. If there are any blocks or obstacles you feel about achieving your goals, it can be a good idea to first create a releasing ritual on the night of a full moon, which is a powerful time for getting rid of old habits, thoughts, and beliefs that no longer serve you. Write intentions to release specific beliefs or thoughts, and after declaring your desire to release them, discard the paper you have written on. Once your full moon ritual has been done, you can then prepare for the new moon ritual with your new, positive intentions.

DISPLAYS AND ALTARS

Follow the advice in this book about using crystals in your home or workplace to help with creating displays, both for decorative purposes and intentional purposes. You also can display crystals according to which colors suit your surroundings, to add vibrancy, texture, patterns, and extra beauty to your environment. A great way to experience the power of crystals is to create an altar, which is a display point such as a table or a shelf where a selection of items are placed, to honor something or someone or to gather energy and focus for a particular purpose or intention.

Crystals are wonderful items to include in an altar, especially alongside other items like candles, flowers, photos, decorative items, affirmation cards, incense, essential oils, and symbolic statues. It is a bit like a shrine or a manifestation zone for your desires. You can create a love altar, a health altar, an abundance altar, or a general altar for overall positive vibes. Try creating an altar in the bedroom, living room, or office to focus your intentions for that area.

JEWELRY AND WEARABLE CRYSTALS

There is no better way to experience the benefits of crystals for the body than to wear them against the skin, where they can have a direct effect for a long period of time. Crystal jewelry is popular, and you can either purchase premade jewelry or create your own. There are special spiral holders that can house tumbled stones to create a pendant, or you can find predrilled stones to thread on your own. The good thing about crystal jewelry is you can customize it to suit your specific intentions, either overall for the bigger picture of your life or for particular times such as going for job interviews, getting medical treatment, or looking for a relationship.

Crystals that have an affinity for the heart are great to wear as pendants, crystals for creativity and productivity are perfect as bracelets or rings, and crystals for focus or protection can be good as earrings. The main thing is you are connected to a piece of jewelry and feel good wearing it.

CREATIVITY WITH CRYSTALS

For the creatives among us or those looking to discover their self-expression, crystals can be made into artworks. Although they are beautiful on their own and are perfect examples of nature's built-in artistry, making a piece of crystal art can be an even more beautiful way of harnessing the crystal energy and radiating it to your surroundings. Crystals can enrich your overall imagination by helping you tune in to high-vibration frequencies and universal energy from which unlimited inspiration derives. They also can help to inspire you with the beauty and magic of what is possible, enhancing your creative pursuit or art form in new and unique ways.

To fortify your overall creativity, have these crystals with you: peacock ore, lapis lazuli, carnelian, and celestite.

CRYSTAL ART AND CRAFT IDEAS

Paintings To add a unique element to a painting, try adding small crystal chips or small stones by gluing them on to the surface or hanging crystal pendants from the bottom of a canvas or timber frame as a type of decorative fringing. If using canvas, you may be able to sew crystals on by wrapping string around

them to encase them (rough edges help to hold them in place) and threading through to the back of the canvas to secure.

Mobiles/Wind Chimes   Agate crystal wind chimes are often sold in stores because their intricate line patterns of varying colors make a visually stunning decorative item and they produce a gentle sound. They may break easily though, so they are best not used in areas that are too windy or in children's rooms. To make your own, find predrilled agate slices and hang them with fishing line on to a circular mobile frame. Another way of making a mobile or a crystal wall hanging is to use a piece of driftwood or a twig or stick and hang crystal pendants from it with fishing line or string, or thread on crystal chips or beads, or wrap rough pieces of quartz in thread and then attach to the stick. You also can add other items like feathers, jewelry, beads, ribbons, and tassels.

Dreamcatchers   For this popular craft activity, as in the crystal mobiles, use a circle base and thread or a dreamcatcher kit. Add crystals to the center parts or hang them from ribbons.

Greeting Cards Try creating your own cards by gluing small crystal chips in a pattern or shape or in a random layout to cardboard cards. You can add drawings, paint, or other items like scrapbooking decorations, glitter, and buttons.

Bookmarks Instead of having a ribbon or tassel hanging from the end of a bookmark, you can hang a crystal pendant for a unique look and to add the power of crystals to your reading time, which may help with focus and concentration, memory retention, or overall enjoyment.

VISION BOARDS

A vision board is a visual representation of your dreams and goals in collage format, usually on a piece of cardboard. It is a powerful way not only to clarify your dreams and intentions, but also to stay focused on them and get inspired by seeing the images you love on a daily basis. Crystals can help in two ways:

- You can have your favorite crystals nearby as you work on your vision board, helping you tune in to your inner guidance and find the pictures that are perfect for you. You also can meditate with them beforehand to get into the right frame of mind for creating your board.

- You can incorporate crystals into your vision board by either printing out photos of crystals you want to use and gluing them on, along with other pictures, or getting some small, flattish crystals and gluing them on to the vision board. Just be sure to use a stronger backing material and flatter-shaped crystals or crystal chips. That way you will have the crystal energy within your life vision, helping to enhance the manifesting power.

For example, stick on rose quartz crystals or photos of them if one of your main intentions is to manifest a loving relationship, or adhere citrine and aventurine for abundance goals and good luck.

CRYSTAL GRIDS

Crystal grids are a stunning way to display crystals, both for decorative purposes and for setting a strong intention and focusing energy into it. They usually take the form of a circular pattern, radiating out from the center, and also may contain flowers, leaves, or feathers. They can be made on a round-shaped base such as a cake stand, old clock, plate, tree stump, or a custom-made crystal grid timber base or cloth. You also can print out grid patterns on paper. When combined with the power of sacred geometry, the effects can be enhanced, as these shapes are thought to be symbolic of perfect balance and harmony, through their symmetrical and repetitive designs and structure.

Looking at photos of crystal grids is the best way to learn how to create them. If you do an online search, you will find many variations to inspire you. Use crystals that you feel connected to or that are associated with the intention you would like to set. Crystal grids are best made with only a few select crystals, to have a more targeted focus and purpose. See each chapter in this book for guidance on choosing which crystals to use for your purpose. Use tumbled stones for the radiating "spokes" and/or a circular border, and a generator crystal such as a point, tower, or pyramid in the center to amplify and focus your intention to the universe.

You can use crystal grids in rituals for gratitude, healing, or manifesting. Add incense or essential oils, music or sound bowls, and written intentions, which you can place under the center crystal or under the base. Create your grid and intention ritual on a full moon for releasing negativity or ties to the past, and on a new moon for manifesting dreams (or they can be created at any time as well).

CRYSTAL HEALING AND THERAPY

Because of the positive power of crystals, they can be used as a form of energetic healing therapy alongside other health treatments, by yourself or with a practitioner. Simply using crystals during meditation is a form of crystal healing. But you or a practitioner also can target specific areas of imbalance by focusing the crystal on that area, above the skin or touching it. This requires a calm

state of mind and clear intention, calling on the healing power of source energy and the properties of the crystal to be focused into that area of the body or as an overall well-being enhancer. Because everything is energy and one thing can have an impact on another at an energetic level, crystals have the potential to be of assistance by raising vibrational frequencies in areas of low vibration or sluggishness, or balancing energy where there may be overactivity. And one of the best healing effects of crystals is on your emotions. Because emotions can influence health situations, dealing with emotional contributors and balancing emotional states with the help of crystals can be beneficial.

Apart from seeing a practitioner who incorporates crystals into their natural healing practice, you also can enjoy the benefits of crystal healing at home. An easy way is to have a healing bath: soak in a bathtub filled with essential oils and large crystals, such as rose quartz or clear quartz or crystals for your specific needs (avoiding those that dissolve or shouldn't be used in water, such as selenite, kyanite, or malachite). Let the crystal vibration transfer through the water and into your body. Alternatively, you can first make a crystal elixir with smaller stones and then add this water to the bathtub. An elixir is water that has had a safe crystal immersed in it for several hours. Only make elixirs with nontoxic crystals and those that do not break or fragment easily. Once the crystal has soaked in the water, you can remove the crystal and use the water as a spritzing spray, in a cloth compress, or add it to your bath. You also can buy crystal water bottles that have a safe crystal within, such as amethyst, rose quartz, or tourmaline.

To make use of crystal healing for yourself, you can place crystals directly over areas of concern, either leaving them there while resting or meditating or holding them for a while with your hands. You can hold the crystal still (good for calming and relaxing), or gently pulse it up and down, or side to side, or move it around in circles (good for removing toxins and excess fluid, stimulating circulation, and encouraging better functioning). The crystal can be touching the body or even be held slightly above it. When you use a crystal in this way, visualize the body part doing what you would like it to do: see tense muscles relaxing, blood flow improving, cells becoming stronger at fighting infections or healing from damage, and so on. Your mind is a powerful tool and even more powerful when combined with crystals for healing benefits.

READINGS AND CRYSTAL COMMUNICATION

Crystals can be a great adjunct to intuitive and psychic readings for yourself or for others. You do not have to be an experienced psychic or healer. We all have the ability to tune in to our intuition and seek insight and answers, and crystals can help as a focal point and an energy amplifier, absorber, and transmitter. They are living and vibrating parts of nature and the universe, and their naturally high frequencies are impacted by their environment, absorbing energy and responding to energy. Thoughts are energy, too, as are feelings and intentions, and through our thought energy we can communicate with crystals and they can communicate with us, when we learn how to tune in and listen.

If you are an experienced intuitive reader or healer, try incorporating crystals if you have not already, either having one crystal that you program as your "reading crystal," which helps you to receive insight and pass on accurate guidance (making sure to cleanse it between readings), or having your client hold a crystal during the reading, which you then take hold of to assist with tuning into their energy.

For everyone else, try selecting one crystal to be your intuition crystal—perhaps a piece of amethyst, quartz, labradorite, or any other crystal you feel drawn to. Cleanse it and program it with the intention that it be used for your highest good in receiving accurate and helpful intuitive insight. Then practice by holding it, taking a few deep breaths, and asking your intuition or your spirit guides a question. Listen and feel for an answer, and jot down any information that you receive. You can get into the habit of doing this each morning by asking, "What do I need to know for today?" to help prepare you for the day ahead. Do not judge any information you receive. Just make a mental or written note, stay aware and open, and check in periodically with your daily insights to see if they are helping you. But do not overthink it.

Oracle cards and tarot cards are also great tools to use with crystals to gain insight into overall life or a specific situation. Choose a crystal to work with, lay it on top of the card deck, and ask for its assistance with the right card at this time. Then shuffle the cards and make your selection. There are even crystal card decks that can help you in intuitively selecting a crystal that may be suited to you right now. Another way of using crystals with card readings is to shuffle and select five cards and lay them down in a row. Then hold your crystal in your hand and move your hand over the cards, asking for it to pause over the best card for you. Move your hand where it feels compelled to go, and stop when it feels right.

To practice receiving insight and communicating with crystal energy, try the Crystal Mind Map activity:

On a sheet of paper or in a notebook, write a crystal name in the middle of the page (or attach a photo of the crystal). Or even better, place the actual crystal on the paper. Then write around it any messages that you receive. Focus on the crystal while holding your pen, and ask it what messages it has for you today. Try to obtain at least four words or themes that you feel the crystal is giving you to focus on. Then go deeper, if you wish, with more specific insight. Use this technique as a channel for spiritual wisdom to flow through to you via the crystal.

An example might be celestite.

* Four words/themes: acceptance, initiative, trust, confidence
* Going deeper, the messages might be:

Accept what is going on around you, and accept other people as doing the best they can.

Take *initiative* in resolving conflicts by showing your understanding and acceptance and acting first with love.

Trust that all is being worked out for you at a higher level; know that the outcome will be just right.

Have *confidence* in your ability to communicate with others and with the universe. You are being heard.

Give the process a try with two or three crystals
you feel drawn to, or use the name of a crystal
you do not have but that comes to mind for you.
Note what the four words are, and then go deeper
to see if you can discover exactly what the crystal
is trying to tell you and what insight is most
beneficial for you or your client at this point.

As you can see, there are a multitude of ways in which you can
benefit from the power of crystals. Read through the following
chapters for targeted guidance on which crystals to use and how to
use them for different areas, purposes, and situations of your life.

1 PHYSICAL HEALTH

Supporting Your Physical Body

It goes without saying that health is one of our most important assets, if not the most important. It would be rare to go through life without some sort of health issue because interacting with our environment invariably exposes us to many possible opportunities for disruptions—infections, chemicals, pollution, electromagnetic radiation, stress, injuries, diet- and lifestyle-related impacts, and genetic contributors. So if we cannot eliminate our exposure completely and apart from treating an issue medically or naturally, the best thing we can do is enhance our body's ability to prevent, adapt to, and deal with what may occur. Health is not the absence of disease; it is a state of balance between mind, body, and spirit, and the ability to handle and recover from disruptions.

The physical body requires nourishment not only from our *environment* (through food, water, sunshine) and our *lifestyle habits* (sleep, exercise, social interaction, and connection), but also from our *energetic source*. The energy that flows through all things, including us, is always present. Yet we can resist its efficient flow at times through negative habits, unhealthy environmental exposure, or unhelpful thoughts and emotions. So the way to support physical health is to target all these contributors to good health and not only one, such as diet. Good health requires an overall and comprehensive approach.

How Can Crystals Support My Physical Health?

Crystals are, at their core, an energetic influence on our energy flow and vibrational frequency, thereby having an impact on one of the contributing supporters of good health. They are not the one and only source of healing, but a complement to other factors. Crystals can assist your health by helping your cells vibrate at a healthier frequency and by directing energy to where it is needed most. They allow you to focus your positive thoughts and intentions into a particular part of the body or the body overall so that you receive this life-enhancing energy and the vibrations that resonate with healthier functioning. Crystals also help via their emotional contribution to health, bringing about happier emotions and clearing any negativity that may have built up. Crystals are a wonderful filter between the outside world and your cells and a powerful amplifier of positive energy from their inner vibrations into your cells.

Which Crystals Are Good for Enhancing Health and Healing?

The crystals used for your health often depend on which health issues you are facing. However, there are some crystals that are good all-rounders for improving your physical and emotional well-being.

Five crystals that can help enhance your health and the healing process are unakite, mookaite, jade, turquoise, and amber.

UNAKITE

Easily recognizable by its contrasting green and orangey-pink patches, this crystal is a great choice for supporting overall health as well as transforming negative energy buildup from the past into the present so that it can be released and removed. It helps to release attachment to past illnesses so that they need not be part of the present reality.

Unakite can support the body when physical conditions are affecting the overall functioning of organs, help the body's energy to realign to a vibration that is more nourishing, and encourage cell regeneration and healing. In addition, it is a strong link between the physical and spiritual, assisting with psychic experiences and restoration on a spiritual level.

* Support for physical health and healing
* Support for male and female reproductive health
* Psychic enhancement
* Releasing the past

꙾ **Affirmation for Unakite** ꙾
"My body is strong and balanced."

MOOKAITE

Also known as "Australian jasper," this beautiful stone with smooth, curving color combinations of earthy-red, orangey-yellow, and brown resembles the Australian outback landscape. It is filled with strong earth energy to support grounding and stability in the body and mind, while also being a link to past and future, instilling wisdom in the body to allow for tuning into cellular energy and helping with intuitive evaluation of health. Mookaite is valuable for wound healing and immune system health and for regenerating cells and tissues.

* Physical health and recovery
* Transmission of healing wisdom
* Adaptability to changing circumstances
* Link between physical and spiritual, past and future

☙ Affirmation for Mookaite ❧
"I enjoy good health in mind, body, and spirit."

JADE

Jade is a calming and healing stone. It comes in varying colors, but it is most often recognized as a muted light-green stone with some darker variations and a soapy appearance. Some specimens have dark veins and reddish-brown patches. Jade is known for bringing good luck and opportunities and is also an integrator of mind and body. It helps with physical healing while encouraging the mind to be more positive and impacting health in that way too. When the body needs soothing and love and positivity, jade is a good choice.

- Good-luck stone
- Positive opportunities and connections
- Stress relief
- Healing and cleansing from negative energy

~ **Affirmation for Jade** ~
"Each new day brings me renewed health and vitality."

TURQUOISE

Often known as a master healer, turquoise is a very valuable crystal that can enhance health and healing on all levels (physical, emotional, and spiritual). It brings all contributors to health issues to light, allowing you to understand how the past has affected your current situation and how your own beliefs and habits may be affecting it also, while assisting with releasing those negative influences. Turquoise is a great strengthener of mind, body, and spirit. It helps all parts to work together in harmony as a whole. It is helpful for health issues where there is a deep emotional or spiritual cause. It allows you to listen to and act on your soul's calling to better serve your life and your health, by encouraging you to live without fear of self-expression.

- Master healer
- Protective and supportive
- Spiritual cleanser
- True, soulful expression

Power Point . . . Authentic turquoise is a greenish-blue and often has darker-colored veins. There are some "fake" turquoise stones on the market that are a brighter aqua-green color, usually made by dyeing white howlite, so be sure you are buying real turquoise and not an imitation. There is also Tibetan turquoise, which is slightly different in properties and color, with more of a green tinge.

☙ Affirmation for Turquoise ❧
"My body has all it needs to be vibrantly healthy."

AMBER

A warm golden-yellowy-brown color, amber contains soothing energy from the earth and trees, bringing negativity and waste to the surface to be removed and flushing away toxins and inflammation. It encourages self-healing of the body, transmitting the right frequency for ideal functioning and regeneration and dealing with pain. It is helpful for when physical issues are caused by or made worse by a negative or low state of mind, lifting and brightening the mind-set so that the body can respond accordingly. Amber is a grounding stone, alleviating feelings of being overwhelmed and disconnection by restoring awareness and links to earth energy and strength.

- Physical cleanser and detoxifier
- Encourages the body's healing systems
- Uplifts the mood
- Grounds the body and mind

Power Point . . . Although it looks like a crystal and has crystal-like properties, amber is technically a solidified resin that comes from trees. It is not uncommon to find amber with insects or plant remnants trapped inside like a fossil.

☙ Affirmation for Amber ❧
"My body is clean, healthy, and stable."

How Can I Use These Crystals for My Health?

Create a crystal "health kit" or sachet containing the recommended crystals, and use them as needed whenever any health challenges occur. Give these as gifts to loved ones who may be suffering. They can simply keep them close or use them more proactively.

Wear an amber beaded necklace or bracelet. This can be good for children, too, or a mother can wear it while holding or breastfeeding her baby. Just be sure it is authentic amber and not an imitation.

Use a jade crystal massage roller or skin roller to gently massage any areas of concern. This can be particularly helpful for aches and pains, poor circulation, and some skin conditions.

Invest in a hot stone massage that uses jade, warmed up to be placed on your body or massaged into muscles.

Hold a unakite crystal to any area that needs assistance, asking the power of source energy to work through it and transmit its healing frequencies to your cells.

Carry turquoise with you to any medical appointments to give you strength, overall healing, and divine support. Black tourmaline and black obsidian also protect against negative influences and bring truth to light, to help in understanding what is going on in your body and what it needs.

Meditate with mookaite, especially if you are recovering from an illness or surgery or if you are unsure what is causing a health imbalance. Do a body scan, slowly moving the mookaite around your body or resting still and focusing your awareness on different parts. Ask it to give you insight into what may be going on and to respond via extra warmth or pulsing vibration in response to different areas you either hold it against or focus on with your thoughts.

Crystal Activities for Physical Health and Healing

1. Health Intention

Write a letter to the universe, your spirit guides, God, or any other spiritual or higher being or energy you feel connected to, and state any concerns you may have about your health. Ask for what you would like . . . whether it be a good outcome, recovery, answers, progress, or awareness of the lessons a challenge is there to teach you. Always ask with gratitude, not neediness, and request that what is in your best and highest good be allowed to manifest. Sometimes a health issue will not go away until we learn what it is trying to teach us and then act on it to make any changes or start a new way of being. So rather than focusing on "getting rid" of something, focus on what you need to know and learn so that it can serve its higher purpose and you can have the best chance of moving forward in better health.

When your letter is complete, place it on an uncluttered table or shelf and surround it with small crystals, such as the ones suggested earlier in this chapter. Place your hands above the letter and crystals and take three deep breaths, feeling the energy being drawn up into your hands. Then read your letter out loud. Hold your hands to your heart afterward and say "thank you." You also may like to light a candle or diffuse some essential oils. You can burn the letter or fold it up and toss it away to symbolically release it to the universe, or you can keep it.

2. Health Crystal Grid

Make a crystal grid (see pages 21–22) containing healing crystals and/or those specific to your needs or that you feel drawn to. For example, try a clear quartz point for the center, along with a piece of turquoise or mookaite, surrounded by radiating stones of unakite, amber, jade, and clear quartz. You can add some sprigs or leaves of fresh herbs such as oregano or rosemary or thyme for their healing properties. Set an intention for your grid (your health intention letter could be a good place to start), light a candle, and ask that these crystals hold and direct your intention to the power of the universe. Keep your grid on display somewhere you can look at it and tune in to it regularly, such as on a nightstand, bookcase, dresser, coffee table, or a plate in the bathroom. Believe and know that this grid is continually working for you to enhance your health.

3. Healing Visualization

One of the best things you can do for your health is to engage in a regular daily meditation and visualization practice. Think of "meditation as your daily medication": a regular dose that allows you to function at your best and cope better with any challenges that come your way.

Choose crystals to use and either place them on or next to body areas that need extra healing, or hold crystals in your hands as you relax, either seated or lying down.

Breathe slowly, and with each exhalation imagine any negative energy leaving your body. Then, visualize positive energy and healing vibes coming into you through your breath and through the crystals. See this flow of energy bathing all your cells in love and well-being. After a while, direct your focus to any parts of the body that are in need of healing or some extra love. Feel the restorative power of the crystal energy drenching every part of your cells in that area and the cells functioning at their best. Now, visualize yourself somewhere you love. Where are you, and what are you doing? How are you feeling? Notice all the details and dwell on the positive emotions it brings. See yourself as complete, healthy, and at peace. Smile and know that you are being looked after and that you have unlimited resources for health and healing available to you at any time. Thank your crystals for their input, and return to your day when ready.

4. Use the affirmations listed for each crystal whenever you need to enhance your health, whether you have the crystal or not.

2 EMOTIONAL WELL-BEING

The Importance of Emotional Well-Being

Good health is not just physical. Mental and emotional health is just as important and impacts our physical health, and vice versa. With increasing awareness around mental health these days, it is becoming a less taboo subject. And with more people being open about their issues and/or needs, there is more support in the community for those affected or those going through difficult life situations. Changing emotions are a natural part of life for all of us, and learning about tools to assist with our emotional well-being is something we can all benefit from.

How Can Crystals Support My Emotions?

Crystals are natural emotion supporters. Through their subtle yet powerful balancing vibrations, they can have an influence on the vibrational energy behind various emotions and allow them to transform when needed, to move through and beyond into a different frequency and state that allows for greater well-being. Emotions should not be blocked; they should be processed and expressed in a healthy way. Crystals can help by allowing deeper awareness, receiving insight into what is going on underneath it all, and highlighting how to move forward. They can assist by making things clearer in your mind and calming any overactivity in the

nervous system, so you can make appropriate choices for your well-being. Specific crystals resonate more with certain emotions, so once you know which crystals are good for a particular emotion or need, you can choose the one most suited to your situation. For example, if you are in need of feeling calm and serene, lepidolite can help. If you feel overwhelmed and require security and groundedness, red jasper is a good choice.

Which Crystals Are Good for Emotional Well-Being?

Crystals will help you to feel more emotionally balanced in general, but some are more specific for particular emotions and issues, such as fear, overwhelm, anxiety, or sadness.

Amethyst and quartz are good starting points for general emotional support, but six other crystals that are particularly helpful with targeted benefits are peach selenite, lepidolite, rose quartz, citrine, red jasper, and obsidian.

PEACH SELENITE

This orange-colored crystal is filled with loving earth energy and light from the spiritual realm and is an overall emotional cleanser. For times of turmoil, grief, and overwhelm, peach selenite is there to show you that it is okay to feel what you are feeling, while also helping you move through these emotions and into a greater peace and freedom.

What is great about the energy in this crystal is that it is not just for soothing emotions or helping you feel better; it works at a level of total transformation, from deep beginnings of emotions through to their current manifestation. It is a transition stone, pulling you out of that deeply rooted past of confusion and trauma, through the necessary process of acknowledging and releasing its hold on you, and into a new state of complete awareness and feelings of acceptance and peace.

Just like biting into a fresh, juicy peach when you are hungry and thirsty, peach selenite will quench your need for emotional relief.

- Brings light to dark situations
- Emotional transitions
- Emotional cleansing
- Peace and acceptance

To help you fully embrace the power of peach selenite for emotional well-being, read this message as though it is coming from a treasured friend.

Dear Courageous Soul,

You have been through a lot. You have gone through more than you thought you should ever experience, but you are still here. You are strong, and you are valuable. See your worth, and allow yourself to fill with love from within.

I am here to help you move through this emotional transition and see you through to greater well-being. It is there for you, ready when you are. Do not hide your emotions or suppress your heart's needs. Allow them to come to the surface and be felt, expressed, released. Through releasing, you will be cleansed and free and ready for a new way of being that will enrich your life and bring you peace.

Love and light,

Peach Selenite

≈ Affirmation for Peach Selenite ≈
*"I make peace with my emotions and move forward
to welcome emotional well-being into my life."*

LEPIDOLITE

The crystal of serenity, lepidolite has a unique and subtle beauty with its soft pinky-lilac hues. It can be used as a tumbled stone or in slices or shards with a glassy appearance and fragility. Mineral-rich in constitution, it contains lithium, one of the ingredients in mood-stabilizing medicines. Lepidolite helps when you feel stuck or trapped by your emotions and negative patterns, and allows your difficulties to be seen with new eyes and a healthier perspective. It will assist with clear thinking, take away excessive thoughts and overwhelming emotions, and calm your nervous system, especially before sleep. It is great for work-related stress in a high-technology environment, because it helps to balance out the effects of electromagnetic frequencies with stabilizing and calming ones. Lepidolite is a soul soother.

- Calming and serene
- Stabilizing and settling, especially before sleep
- Clear thinking and planning
- Balancing effect in a high-technology environment

绔 **Affirmation for Lepidolite** 绕
"Serenity washes through my mind and body.
I am safe and secure."

ROSE QUARTZ

This light-pink crystal is easy to find and well-known for its gentle yet powerful vibration of love: love for the self, for life, and for others. It is suitable for all genders, yet embodies a feminine tenderness and caring energy that nurtures and supports, especially during times of distress. Rose quartz encourages unconditional love, bringing with it a sense of peace and acceptance. It reminds you to start with yourself, to embody the qualities of love, and to radiate this wherever you go. It also allows you to heal from past hurts and emotional difficulties, especially those rooted in fear, bringing clarity and knowledge that love always wins and is always present in life.

- ☀ Love of self and others
- ☀ Peace and acceptance
- ☀ Emotional healing
- ☀ Dissolving of fear (the opposite of love)

☞ Affirmation for Rose Quartz ☜
"The power of love heals and supports me through all emotional states."

CITRINE

This crystal comes in varying depths of yellow (with bits of white), from light and bright to a deep, earthy, yellow-mustard color. The stronger the color, the better, when it comes to its powerful properties. Citrine is a "happy" stone for bringing sunshine and abundance into your life. It is a natural attractor of positive opportunities, and when it is paired with your intentions, it can be a powerful part of your manifesting strategies. It is particularly helpful for bringing good thoughts, instead of worry, so use this stone when there is excess stress in your life. Other benefits include its cleansing effects on your body and the environment and its stimulating impact on creativity and joy, helping to enhance emotional well-being from within.

- ☀ Attractor of abundance and positive opportunities
- ☀ Happiness and joy

※ Cleansing and balancing

※ Energizing and brightening of the mind and body

ॐ **Affirmation for Citrine** ॐ
*"My inner being is filled with joy and happiness,
and this radiates into every area of my life."*

RED JASPER

This earthy-red crystal is a solid-looking stone with properties that enhance the feeling of stability and security. All jasper crystals have a grounding effect and nurture the body while stabilizing the emotions. Red jasper alleviates loneliness and disconnectedness, brings feelings of safety and belonging, and helps you to see the unity of all people and your place in the world. Emotionally, it brings strength during times of hardship and fluctuation, allowing a natural balance to occur and settling overactive responses. With its stabilizing effects, it supports endurance and the ability to keep going and to withstand the effects of chronic stress, and brings forth a consistency of determination and strength.

※ Grounding and security

※ Stabilizes the emotions

※ Supports feelings of belonging and connection

※ Balancing and settling effects

ॐ **Affirmation for Red Jasper** ॐ
*"I am stable and grounded within myself
and the world around me."*

OBSIDIAN

A glossy black stone, obsidian is very strong and powerful when it comes to absorbing and releasing energy and bringing out the truth. It is protective, but it is also honest and open, allowing you to see things for exactly what they are and discovering underlying causes to various situations and emotional upheavals. It gives you the gift of knowledge and awareness, so you can make decisions and changes to better align with what you want.

Obsidian is helpful when there are things that need releasing or letting go of. But, first, they must come to the surface, and obsidian helps with this as well. If you are ready for removing blocks and living with full, authentic, raw, and honest truth, then obsidian is the crystal for you. It is especially helpful on a full moon.

- Exposing the truth
- Bringing fears and blocks to the surface to be released
- Protection
- Authenticity

Power Point . . . Obsidian was formed from the rapid cooling of molten lava, which gave it a glassy appearance. Its rapid formation is said to be behind its strong and powerful energetic properties.

☙ Affirmation for Obsidian ❧
"With the truth, I set myself free from all limitations."

How Can I Use These Crystals for My Emotional Well-Being?

Wear a red jasper bracelet or keep a small piece in your pocket to help you stay grounded while out and about.

Keep a citrine cluster or tumbled stone somewhere you will see it each morning when getting ready for the day ahead, to remind you that you can be happy and have the power to bring sunshine into the lives of others.

Meditate with lepidolite and rose quartz to help you feel more serene and loving toward yourself and others.

During times of stress, **hold on to a peach selenite crystal** and take several deep breaths, allowing them to calm your worries and bring more peace of mind.

Crystal Activities for Emotional Well-Being

1. Peaceful Meditation

   Find a peaceful piece of music or a guided audio meditation that you like, and create a ritual around it. You can set an intention to have a calming experience by holding one of the suggested crystals or any crystal you feel drawn to, and then lay it beside you or somewhere on your body (on your heart or forehead is a good place or simply in your hands). Sometimes life requires us to surrender to what is going on, not try to fix anything, and just focus on our inner experience, so we can cope better and prioritize our well-being. Having a regular meditation or relaxation practice (whether it is ten, twenty, or thirty minutes) gives us a sense of security within ourselves and something to look forward to, knowing that no matter what is going on around us, we have our daily practice to recenter us.

2. **Emotional Release Process**

   Sometimes for our emotional well-being we need to allow
   ourselves to feel something first and then let it go. Using
   a crystal such as peach selenite, which has an emotional
   cleansing effect, acknowledge your emotions. Holding the
   crystal, say (out loud preferably) how you are feeling. Ask
   the crystal to help you process this emotional state and say
   that you would like help in releasing any emotions that are
   not serving you. Hold the crystal to your heart, and with
   each exhalation imagine these emotions being drawn into
   the crystal. Then imagine them being transferred out the
   other side and into the universe to be dissolved, or leave the
   crystal in the sun or moonlight to cleanse the crystal and
   release the emotional vibrations.

3. **Flip the Emotional Switch**

   Acknowledge how you are actually feeling, and then
   think about what emotion you would like to feel. It may
   be the opposite of your current state, or it may be just a

small step forward so that the transition is not as intense or unrealistic. Sometimes jumping to the opposite right away can feel too challenging, so it can be easier to work your way through bit by bit. For example, you could go from anger to acceptance, or anger to calm, or even anger to understanding. When you have decided what feels better and achievable, choose a crystal that will resonate with your desired emotion or state of being. If you want to go from fear to love, you could choose rose quartz or rhodochrosite. There are many options for different emotional desires, and the crystals mentioned in the previous section are some suggestions that may assist with common ones.

When experiencing an upheaval that you do not want to continue with, remember: flip the switch by acknowledging what you are feeling and then decide what you want instead. This alone will help raise your vibration, and using an appropriate crystal will help even further.

4. Crystal Helper

Choose a crystal you feel drawn to, preferably one that is associated with peace and clarity and love, and make it your designated crystal helper. Carry it with you in your pocket or purse, briefcase, car, or anywhere you can have easy access to it. Whenever you are faced with a decision, especially one with an emotional component, check in with your inner guidance and crystal helper to make a decision that is best for you. Hold your crystal and ask, "What is the decision that will be best for myself at this time [and for all involved, if others will be impacted]?" Listen for what feels right, and trust it. Accept this crystal helper as your friend, who is there whenever needed, to assist you in making choices that benefit your emotional well-being and your life. This process also trains you to use your intuition.

5. **Complementary Tools and Tips to Assist with Emotional Well-Being**

Essential oils also can be great for impacting your emotions. *Try patchouli* for grounding, *clary sage* to soothe and balance mood, and *bergamot* for anxiety.

Try daily journaling to acknowledge and express your feelings and honor your emotions.

Gratitude is one of the best emotional balancers because it puts your focus on the positive in every situation. Write down three things each day that you are grateful for, no matter what else is going on.

Healing therapies like *reiki and massage* can assist with emotional support, while also providing physical benefits.

6. **Use the affirmations listed for each crystal whenever you need to feel more emotional well-being, whether you have the crystal or not.**

3 SELF-LOVE

What Is Self-Love and Why Is It Important?

Self-love is about love, honor, and respect for yourself. It is about accepting who you are—your strengths and your weaknesses—and loving yourself regardless. Self-love is unconditional. It is not "I will love myself when I am my ideal body weight" or "I only love myself when I am helping others." It is loving yourself when you do not feel perfect or at your best, and even when you are saying no to others. In fact, saying no is sometimes a perfect act of self-love, when you know that your needs must come first in certain situations. Self-love is an important starting point for all the other wonderful things in your life. When you love and accept yourself first, you are more able to love and accept others, have more to give, and will find yourself attracting more love and acceptance of yourself from others too.

What Does Self-Love Look Like in Life?

It is not just shown in getting massages and facials, exotic travel, or buying a new outfit, although these things can be acts of self-love. True self-love goes deeper. It involves changing your inner thoughts and dialogue to be more loving and accepting. It involves an ongoing understanding of yourself and your needs, your boundaries, your dreams and passions, and your priorities.

It involves acting on these needs and boundaries and staying strong in yourself and what is right for you, regardless of what others expect of you. True self-love is listening to your body, your heart, and your soul, and making what really matters to you your top priority. This can be shown outwardly by spending more time on things you enjoy, being around people who lift you up and accept who you are, not trying to be a superhero, switching off your phone when you need to wind down and connect with yourself, prioritizing your sleep, and making self-care practices part of your daily life.

How Can Crystals Enhance My Sense of Self-Love?

If you want to enhance the love you feel for yourself or tune in more deeply to the love within you, crystals are a great tool. With their high vibrational frequencies, they naturally embody the essence of love, some more so than others. Their energy can impact yours in a way that allows you to reset your vibration to one of alignment and love. Crystals are naturally beautiful things, and it is easy to love them. Some crystals are not as visually appealing but are more interesting than beautiful. Yet they are still high in vibration of love. They can be reminders to us that not everything has to look or be perfect to be lovable. We are human beings, all different, yet all the same. Crystals are like this too. They can teach us to love our differences, uniqueness, and authenticity. They are also a physical way to focus intentions and express ourselves through combining thoughts, words, and feelings with our sense of sight and touch, as well as our sixth sense on an energetic level.

Which Crystals Are Good for Self-Love?

The properties of certain crystals can enhance various aspects of self-love. They can help you tune in to energy that embodies acceptance, peace, empowerment, communication—all different aspects involved in self-love.

Four crystals that are especially helpful for boosting and embracing a sense of self-love are rose quartz, aventurine, larimar, and rhodochrosite.

ROSE QUARTZ

This light-pink crystal is easy to find and well-known for its gentle yet powerful vibration of love: love for the self, for life, and for others. It is suitable for all genders, yet embodies a feminine tenderness and caring energy that nurtures and supports. Rose quartz encourages unconditional love, bringing with it a sense of peace and acceptance. It reminds you to start with yourself, to embody the qualities of love, and to radiate this wherever you go. It also allows you to heal from past hurts and emotional difficulties, bringing clarity and knowledge that love always wins and is always present in life.

- Love of self and others
- Peace and acceptance
- Emotional healing
- Dissolving of fear (the opposite of love)

To help you fully embrace the power of rose quartz for self-love, read this message as though it is coming from a treasured friend.

Dear Loving Being,

You are loved, loving, and lovable. Always remember that love is your source and your power; it is an ongoing gift you can enjoy at any time, anywhere. There is no limit to the love in your life. It is the life force that keeps you going and that connects us all. Love is who we are, and you are part of the greater energy of love that extends beyond time and space.

I am here to remind you of the love that you are, the love that you deserve, and the love you have to share. I am supporting you in your emotional healing and helping you feel more at peace with who you are and what your life is about. Think of me whenever you need to remember your true inner power—the power of love—and always remember to act with love, speak with love, and, first and foremost, love yourself.

Love,

Rose Quartz

➤ **Affirmation for Rose Quartz** ✧
"I am loving, lovable, and loved. I am love."

AVENTURINE

This light-green stone correlates to the heart chakra and therefore embodies love, along with rose quartz, while also strengthening the heart. It is known as a stone of good luck and prosperity, bringing natural, calm confidence and positive outcomes. For self-love, this crystal encourages strength and resilience in matters of the heart and helps you feel a calm sense of peace within, as well as releasing negative emotions about the self.

- Heart chakra strengthener
- Clears negative feelings
- Boosts self-esteem and confidence
- Brings new, positive perceptions

❧ Affirmation for Aventurine ❦
*"I am lucky and blessed to be who I am.
I love and accept myself."*

LARIMAR

This beautiful stone with colors of the Caribbean Sea is a strong feminine crystal of empowerment, taking self-love even higher and connecting the heart to others. With its goddess energy, it helps you to break free of limiting beliefs about yourself so that you can gain a positive and loving new perspective about who you are, inspiring others in the process to love themselves and the beauty of life.

- Feminine earth goddess energy
- Transformative

- Heart healing
- Self-empowerment and love

Power Point . . . Larimar is found only in the Dominican Republic, making it a highly prized stone for crystal lovers. It is known as "the Atlantis stone" because the region in which it is found is said to be part of the lost city of Atlantis.

> ⭐ Affirmation for Larimar ⭐
> *"I lovingly embrace and express the beauty of who I am."*

RHODOCHROSITE

This multilayered crystal with red, pink, and earthy-white and gray hues holds an energetic vibration of universal and unconditional love. It helps to open the heart to love and allow true love to be freely expressed. Associated with the rose, it embodies the delicate energy of love and beauty and allows for deep healing to take place emotionally for all matters of the heart, including past trauma that has affected one's feelings of worthiness. It helps to move beyond the past, accept all emotions, and love oneself unconditionally.

- Unconditional love for self and others
- Loving communication and expression
- Helps accept and clear past trauma
- Brings lightness, playfulness, and love

> ⭐ Affirmation for Rhodochrosite ⭐
> *"I am part of the universal, unconditional love*
> *that is present in the world."*

How Can I Use These Crystals for Self-Love?

Keep them close to you, put in pockets, or wear as jewelry. Hold them as needed to focus your energy and intentions.

Rose quartz is great for the bedroom, especially in the relationship corner if you are interested in the benefits of feng shui. Heart-shaped rose quartz is even better if you want to attract romantic love. A crystal sphere radiates more love into your surroundings, which is good for existing relationships.

Larimar is good to hold or keep in your pocket or on your desk if you need to communicate lovingly and with self-respect and empowerment.

Tumbled or polished rhodochrosite makes a wonderful jewelry piece because of its beautiful layers of different shades of pink, and it helps you feel empowered, loving, and connected to universal love.

Crystal Activities for Self-Love

Do the crystal activities listed below to make the most of your crystals.

1. **Heart Chakra Meditation**
   Hold a rose quartz and/or an aventurine crystal to your heart while seated, or lay them on your chest while lying down. Take three deep breaths to relax. Then with each subsequent breath, imagine your heart chakra filling with love energy from these crystals. Feel your heart becoming lighter and lovelier and radiating love throughout your body and then

around you and into the world. Maintain the meditation for as long as you like or simply do this technique for a few moments regularly throughout the day to keep your heart chakra open and balanced.

2. **Body Gratitude Process**
Using a green aventurine stone, stand in front of a mirror and hold the stone to any body parts that you feel discomfort or dislike about, whether it be physical appearance or function. Take a breath and say, "I now release any negative thoughts or feelings held here." Then take another breath and imagine them dissolving, before moving the stone to any other parts. If you do not feel any obvious dislike or discomfort anywhere, simply hold the stone to your heart and say, "I now release any subconscious limiting beliefs."

Next, take the rose quartz and hold it to each body part from before, this time saying out loud what you love about it, whether it is simple or complex, visual or functional. For example, "I love that my skin holds my body together," or "I love how my legs help me walk," or "I love how my smile lines show how much I've laughed in my life."

Now, hold a larimar crystal to your heart and say, "I lovingly embrace and express the beauty of who I am."

If you have a piece of rhodochrosite jewelry, put it on and remind yourself that you are a loving, lovable, and loved being and part of the universal love.

3. **Self-Love Expression Board**
Make a self-love expression board, just like a vision board or dream board, which is a visual display of positive pictures

and words that show your love for your true, authentic self. When complete, display this board somewhere you will see it regularly, such as near your bedroom or bathroom mirror.

To make one, find a piece of cardboard or strong paper and cut out pictures that resonate with who you are and what you love, along with words that express your positive traits and gifts (or write these directly on the board). For example, *kind, helpful, great smile, resilient, healthy,* and *loving.*

To add crystal power to your board, find pictures online of the crystals you love or the four detailed in this section and print them out to stick to your board. Alternatively, if you can find real crystals that are small and not too heavy, glue them on to the board so that the energy of these crystals will add extra power to your self-love expression.

4. Complementary Tools to Use with These Crystals

Roses or petals: buy a bunch of roses or a single one and place near your self-love board or next to your crystals, or use rose petals for a self-love bath. You also can put rose quartz crystals in the bathwater; just do not let them wash away!

Essential oils: rose, rose geranium, jasmine, lavender. Use these in a diffuser to enhance love vibes around you or in a massage oil for helping with self-love of your body.

Clear quartz crystal can amplify the effects of all crystals and has a great affinity with rose quartz. Use clear quartz crystal alongside rose quartz whenever needed, or keep one next to your crystals.

5. Use the affirmations listed for each crystal whenever you need a self-love boost, whether you have the crystal or not.

$\displaystyle 4$ HEALTHY RELATIONSHIPS

What Constitutes a Healthy Relationship?

A healthy relationship, whether a romantic partnership or a friendship, is one where both people feel accepted and understood, heard and respected. It is based on mutual love and support, encouragement, and allowing the other person to be who they are without judgment. A healthy relationship also allows for forgiveness, listening to each person, and validating what they are feeling so that conflicts can be resolved with peace and acceptance and a deeper respect, which make the relationship grow.

Some relationships last for life and others for shorter periods of time, depending on the nature of the relationship and the purpose and how each person responds and grows. Although it is important to maximize your relationships and do your best to honor both yourself and the other person, it is sometimes important to let certain relationships go or change form if they have served their purpose.

How Can Crystals Support My Relationships?

Crystals can support your relationships by enhancing harmonious vibrations and providing clarity and insight, as well as helping to come from a place of love in decisions and conflicts. They can remind you to trust your inner guidance and do what is right for you, ensuring that your relationship with yourself is top priority. Even just having crystals around and noticing them regularly triggers your mind to have healthier perceptions about any challenges and to act and speak with love. They are visual reminders that life is beautiful, if we let it be, and our relationships can be too. They are an energetic influence, acting at an emotional level, to assist us with our interactions and communication.

Which Crystals Are Good for Enriching My Relationships?

You can use crystals specific to your relationship needs, such as for communication, passion, or calming anger and frustration. Or you can utilize those that give off an overall harmonious and loving vibe. Regardless of any particular areas you need to focus on, most issues come down to love, communication, understanding, and harmony or balance.

Four crystals that help with these main relationship issues are amazonite, sodalite, blue lace agate, and rhodochrosite.

AMAZONITE

This beautiful greenish/aqua-colored crystal is wonderful for releasing negative emotions and vibrations in the environment because of its ability to act as a filter. It can sort out physical and emotional negative energy, protect against electromagnetic radiation from home appliances and technology, and help to prevent negative thoughts and emotions becoming dominant through its balancing action. It helps to harmonize relationships through its ability to shift vibrations to the positive side and bring clarity from both perspectives, having a regulating effect on people in the surrounding area. It is a stone of hope, allowing bright possibilities to be illuminated and pursued.

- Protection from negative frequencies
- Balances thoughts and emotions
- Hope and harmony
- Healthy communication

≈ Affirmation for Amazonite ≈
"My relationships are harmonious and healthy."

SODALITE

Sodalite is a blue-and-white-streaked crystal that is perfect for both the physical aspects of home and work environments and the relationship dynamics between friends, family, and colleagues. It can be used for electromagnetic protection from computers and phones, but its main strength lies in its resonance with group dynamics and communication. It helps interactions to be harmonious and accepting and perception to be understanding and wise, and it allows individuals to speak with confidence and loving truth. It unites all in a clear and positive purpose, helping to keep the big picture relevant and front of mind so that you can avoid getting caught up in small issues that distract from a higher divine intent.

- Clearing and calming
- Harmony and teamwork
- Understanding and acceptance
- Confident communication

≈ Affirmation for Sodalite ∾
"I enjoy harmonious and truthful communication
in my relationships."

BLUE LACE AGATE

Blue lace agate is one of the prettiest crystals. As its name suggests, it has a lacelike appearance with layers of curvy banding. Its light-blue colors give off a calming and serene vibe, and the layers are like soothing ripples or waves of music that reach us on a soul level. This crystal helps to support our most important relationship—the one with ourselves. It allows us to go deep within, layer by layer, to reveal underlying patterns and emotional habits that we may have developed over time during difficult situations. These learned responses are stored within and packed on top of one another. And for those that are not serving our best interests, we can begin to release them gradually and

peacefully, with the help of this gentle but powerful crystal, and unravel the layers of our emotional pain and sensitivity.

When we discover and deal with our own issues, we begin to open up to new ways of understanding, not only ourselves but also other people, thereby helping our relationships to thrive. This crystal assists with honest communication via the throat chakra, helping our thoughts and feelings to become clear words and our true selves to be heard and acknowledged and bringing our soul's wisdom out into the open to shine bright.

- Calming and soothing
- Emotional truth and freedom
- Honest communication
- Soulful self-expression

To help you fully embrace the power of blue lace agate for healthy relationships, read this message as though it is coming from a treasured friend.

Dear Unique Soul,

It is time for you to shine. You have many unique gifts to express, and it is safe to bring them out and be seen. It is safe to be who you are and express this fearlessly.

Do not be afraid of your emotional or spiritual journey. You are on the right path, and each layer of awareness and release you go through is moving you further along your true direction. The more you travel this path, the more you step into the power of who you truly are.

Let what has scarred you in the past be what has built up your strength and resilience. Your history is your foundation but not your future. It is the learning point for what is next, and you are ready to move beyond old patterns and fully embrace the beautiful and unique soul that you are. Speak up, express yourself, and live authentically.

Truthfully,

Blue Lace Agate

↣ Affirmation for Blue Lace Agate ↢
"I am safe and supported in expressing my soul's truth."

RHODOCHROSITE

This multilayered crystal with red, pink, and earthy-white and gray hues holds an energetic vibration of universal and unconditional love. It helps to open the heart to love and allow true love to be freely expressed, enhancing relationships. Associated with the rose, it embodies the delicate energy of love and beauty and allows for deep healing to take place emotionally for all matters of the heart, including past trauma that is affecting current relationships. It helps to move beyond the past, accept all emotions, and face all challenges with love and grace. This crystal is a reminder to bring awareness into the present and allow for each person in a relationship to be loved unconditionally.

❋ Unconditional love for self and others

❋ Loving communication and expression

❋ Helps accept and clear past trauma

❋ Brings lightness, playfulness, and love

☙ **Affirmation for Rhodochrosite** ❧
"I love and accept others unconditionally."

How Can I Use These Crystals for Relationships?

Stick a thin piece of amazonite on your phone or phone cover to filter electromagnetic radiation and to help harmonize your conversations.

When you need to talk to someone truthfully without creating conflict, wear a piece of sodalite jewelry, which helps with expression, communication, and harmony.

If you are feeling misunderstood, not accepted, or held back in your relationships when it comes to being your true self, meditate regularly with blue lace agate and place it on your throat chakra. This will help with dealing with past hurts and allow you to express truthfully and peacefully who you really are.

Keep some rhodochrosite in the home for assistance with your living environment relationships, whether they be with a romantic partner, family, or housemates. This crystal gives off loving vibes and reminds us to accept diversity and individual differences.

Give your significant other and yourself one of a pair of the same type of crystal, as a symbol of your connection and bond and commitment to loving each other and communicating with respect. Get the crystals out whenever you need to have an important discussion, and agree to hear each other out and come from a place of love instead of judgment.

Crystal Activities for Healthy Relationships

1. Create a Relationship Altar

When it comes to your romantic relationship (attracting one or enhancing one), a relationship altar can be a great way to honor it as a special and important part of your life. Having this shrine to focus on helps you to stay aligned with what is good about it and what is working, rather than on what is not. It can simply be a corner of a bookcase, a whole shelf, a side table, or two bedside tables. The aim is to make it a focal point for what is positive in the relationship and for what you wish to enhance or attract. Once you have decided on a space, make sure it is clear. You may wish to burn sage around it or cleanse it with carnelian or black tourmaline, combined with your intention, to set a strong foundation for your new altar. Fill the space with things that represent your relationship or symbolize what you want to enjoy and enhance: a photo of the both of you, greeting cards or love notes, special small gifts you have received, a candle with two wicks (or two candles side by side), a vase of fresh flowers, a succulent plant, a painting or print that has a loving feeling, and, of course, some crystals.

Use one or more of the crystals suggested here, any you are drawn to, or, even better, one or two that you both choose. Rose quartz is always a foolproof crystal for relationships. Rhodochrosite can go a little deeper into strengthening your love bond and accepting differences, and blue stones like sodalite and blue lace agate will help with enhancing communication. Selenite can be good to keep things clean and clear. Having two crystal heart shapes is a good idea or some crystal word stones (flattened, round crystals with positive words engraved on them, such as *Love, Forever, Peace*). A crystal sphere can be good, too, to radiate more love around your space and to connect with the energy of the other items on your altar. Bless your altar, when complete, with a prayer of gratitude for what you have and an intention for going forward.

2. **Focus on the Positive Traits**

   Think about all the significant relationships in your life, and for the most important ones, make a list of all their positive traits: the gifts you and the other person bring to it. Use a sheet of paper or one page in a journal for each person or relationship, whether it be your spouse, best friend, colleague, child, sibling, boss, in-law, etc. Write their name at the top and your relationship to them. Then list as many positives as you can. Have a rhodochrosite crystal nearby when writing this list, or hold it for a few moments while tuning in to that person and your relationship until you feel all the value it has in your life and in theirs.

Whenever you have any conflict or difficulties in any
of these relationships, refer back to your lists and remind
yourself of their value. They also can help you to see if any
relationships are changing or evolving to a point where they
no longer have the same purpose, so you can gracefully and
peacefully move on. In most cases, though, this exercise will
help you retain the joy in your relationships by recognizing
and emphasizing what is good about them.

3. Surround Your Relationships with Good Vibes

If you display photos of your family and friends in your
environment, try attaching crystals to some of them. You can
decorate an existing frame by gluing a crystal or crystals on
to it, or you can buy plain photo frames with the intention
of creating little artworks out of them with crystals and
anything else you may like, such as paint, glitter, paper or
wooden shapes, or other decorations. By doing this, you are
infusing crystal energy into the photo and what it represents,
enhancing the high vibrations around this relationship. The
decorated frames also make great gifts for loved ones.

4. Focus on What You Can Give

When going through relationship challenges, flip your focus
from what you are not getting or what you want to get to
what you are getting and what you can give. This is something
you can control, and by doing so, you are more likely to feel
satisfaction in the relationship because you are not dependent
or reliant on someone else to fill your needs. It can help

to write down on paper or jot into a note on your phone the name of the person or relationship and then under the heading "What I can give," what you choose to bring into the relationship. Be certain it is not what you choose to give out of expectation of receiving the same or something else in return, but what you choose to give for the sake and joy of giving it. This is true giving. Just make sure that you give only as an *extension* of yourself, not at the *expense* of yourself. Making sure your relationship with yourself is top priority allows you to feel full with love and eager to give to others, so think, too, about what you choose to give *to* yourself. You will often find that what you give to yourself naturally comes back to you anyway. But let the universe and law of attraction figure that out for you, and take away any expectations or neediness.

For this exercise, imagine that you are the crystal. What benefits would you bring to this relationship? Will you bring love, peace, and acceptance, like rose quartz? Or will you bring listening skills, harmonious responses, understanding, and acknowledgment of another's self-expression, like sodalite? Perhaps your gifts are more physical, like great hugs, smiles and encouragement, and a helping hand with chores and responsibilities when the other person is overworked or overwhelmed. Write down all the things, both in general and specifically, that you will focus on giving, and watch your relationships flourish.

5. Use the affirmations listed for each crystal whenever you need to enhance your relationships, whether you have the crystal or not.

5 ATTRACTING LOVE

What Is Love?

Many people classify love as a feeling, an emotion that we have for someone, and it is that. But love is so much more! Love is the basic foundation of who we are, of our energetic source, which holds everything else together. It is part of all of us, connecting mind, body, and spirit and helping them work together in unity and harmony.

Love really is what makes the world go round, and we are either letting it flow into our lives or resisting it, consciously or subconsciously. Attracting love is not about finding it but about letting it into your life, reducing your resistance to receiving and giving it. It is also about attracting a "love"-based relationship that is a match to your unique self and your desires and that aligns with the life journey you are taking. Getting involved in the right relationship or the one you perceive is right for you can often take a few attempts or sometimes even a lifetime. But if you desire it, then you can receive it.

How Do I "Attract" Love?

To attract love or, more important, love that is healthy and beneficial to both partners, it is important to have a healthy love and respect for yourself. It is also important to remember that your life is a mirror: what you choose to be and who you are will be reflected back at you, so focus on *being* love.

You can make lists of your ideal partner or relationship, traits you would like, and so on, but what is more important is focusing on how you want to *feel* in this relationship and what you are looking forward to *bringing* to this relationship. When you focus more on what you want to *get* out of it, it can become needs-based or create a lot of expectation and pressure and disappointment when the relationship does not meet all those needs. But when you focus on the feelings and the joy and the gifts, you are always in control of your own thoughts and emotions (even though it may not feel like it at times), and therefore remain in the driver's seat of your own life. If another person complements your focus on feelings and you complement theirs, then that is a wonderful thing and is worth pursuing and giving your attention to. That is what you want to attract.

How Can Crystals Help Me Attract and Maintain Love?

Crystals, especially those you feel particularly drawn to, are naturally helping you to clarify your desires and what you are looking for. By choosing a crystal intuitively and from a place of alignment with your true self, you will choose one that suits you and benefits you, more than if you looked for one in a moment of frustration or hurt. The same goes for attracting a loving partner. Come at it from a place of joyful anticipation, rather than neediness or hurt, and you will find a better match for your true self.

Crystals will help you align with that true self and listen to your inner guidance so that you can attract the love you desire. Because love is the basis of everything, crystals come from a place of love, and those high vibrations contained within are natural storers and absorbers and transmitters of love energy. Connect with a crystal, and you are connecting with the power of love *and* the power of crystals.

Which Crystals Are Good for Attracting Love into My Life?

Because all crystals contain love energy, you can choose any one that feels right to you. But there are some crystals that are well-known for their love-enhancing properties, and these are rose quartz, rhodochrosite and rhodonite, garnet, jade, emerald, watermelon tourmaline, and any stones with a pink color or a green color, which resonate with the heart chakra.

ROSE QUARTZ

This light-pink crystal is easy to find and well-known for its gentle yet powerful vibration of love—love for the self, for life, and for others. It is suitable for all genders, yet embodies a feminine tenderness and caring energy that nurtures and supports. Rose quartz encourages unconditional love and worthiness, bringing with it a sense of peace and acceptance of life and of who you are. It reminds you to start with yourself, to embody the qualities of love, and to radiate this wherever you go, knowing that you are deserving of love just the way you are. It also allows you to heal from past hurts and emotional difficulties, bringing clarity and knowledge that love always wins and is always present in life.

- Love of self and others
- Peace and acceptance
- Emotional healing
- Dissolving of fear (the opposite of love)

RHODOCHROSITE

This multilayered crystal with red, pink, and earthy-white and gray hues holds an energetic vibration of universal and unconditional love. It helps to open the heart to love and allow true love to be freely expressed, enhancing relationships and attracting beneficial new partnerships. Associated with the rose, it embodies the delicate energy of love and beauty and allows for deep healing to take place emotionally for all matters of the heart, including past trauma that is affecting current relationships. It helps to move beyond the past, accept all emotions, and face all relationship challenges with love and grace. This crystal is a reminder to bring awareness into the present and appreciate each person for who they are, see the best in those around you, and know that when you unconditionally love yourself, you are aligning with the energy of being unconditionally loved by another.

- Unconditional love for self and others
- Loving communication and expression
- Helps accept and clear past trauma
- Brings lightness, playfulness, and love

❧ Affirmation for Rhodochrosite ❦
*"I am ready to share the immense love
I have within with someone special."*

RHODONITE

With a similar coloring to rhodochrosite, but slightly darker and with blackish flecks, rhodonite is a stone of love. It not only helps you embody and attract love, but also assists with letting go of past hurts, releasing blame, and allowing yourself to forgive. It is helpful when an old relationship created unhealthy attachments or conflicts because it brings a new perspective, so your heart can heal and open up to love again.

Rhodonite is balancing, healing, and supportive, nourishing to the heart chakra, and encouraging of healthy habits.

- Healing from emotional wounds
- Forgiveness of self and others
- Love enhancer
- Balancing

⮞ Affirmation for Rhodonite ⮜
"I release my heart from the past and welcome new love into my life."

GARNET

Most often used is the deep reddish-black crystal known for its warming and nourishing effects that allow the body to rejuvenate and regain passion. It can assist with adding dynamic energy to reproductive organs and reducing stress or lack of desire. It encourages dedication and ardor between partners, strengthening the bond within a new relationship so it can thrive. Garnet is helpful for dating after a period of not dating, because it reignites

confidence to bring out the best version of yourself and attract a
suitable partner.

- ☀ Energy booster
- ☀ Enhances connection, desire, and bonding
- ☀ Strengthening
- ☀ Self-confidence and personal power

> ⌇ Affirmation for Garnet ⌇
> *"I welcome a healthy, passionate
> relationship into my life."*

JADE

Jade is a calming and healing stone. It comes in varying colors, but
it is most often recognized as a muted light-green stone with some
darker variations and a soapy appearance. Some specimens have
dark veins and reddish-brown patches. Jade is known for bringing
good luck, opportunities, and connections. It also is an integrator
of mind and body, helping you with loving thoughts about yourself
and connecting with your heart chakra to embody and attract love.
Jade helps you to remain calm and trusting of your journey to love
and to know that what is right for you is coming.

- ☀ Good-luck stone
- ☀ Stress relief and soothing
- ☀ Nourishes the heart chakra
- ☀ Healing and cleansing from negative energy

❧ Affirmation for Jade ◈
"My heart is calm and pure, supported by loving energy."

EMERALD

Emerald is often cut into a gemstone to make the most of its stunning green color and is also found as a raw crystal that is paler in appearance. It is the crystal to use when longing for a relationship because it strengthens mutual bonds and dedication between lovers, stimulating commitment and loyalty. For this reason, as well as because of its beauty, it is often used in engagement rings. Emerald will help to equalize a relationship so that both partners are satisfied and happy. It can therefore be used where there is an imbalance of power or give-and-take. For attracting love, emerald resonates with the heart chakra and therefore supports love from within, strengthening the self and preparing you for receiving love in your life.

- Commitment and loyalty
- Strengthens the heart and self-love
- Balance and equality
- Clarity and understanding

Power Point . . . Emerald is highly regarded throughout history as a powerful gem and is often worn by royalty and used in religious ceremonies.

❧ Affirmation for Emerald ◈
"I am ready for a loving, committed relationship of equal partners."

WATERMELON TOURMALINE

This crystal combines the colors of pink and green, both resonating with the heart chakra, which makes it extremely valuable for heart-related matters and love. It helps to release old hurt and pain, especially from relationships, and protects against them building up again, allowing a new self to be born. In this way, it is a breaker of patterns that are not serving your highest good. It can be helpful on a full moon to let go of past beliefs, while offering protection against negative cycles recurring.

* Encourages love-based actions
* Heart healing and emotional cleansing
* Recreation and rebirth
* Breaks old patterns

> ᕈ Affirmation for Watermelon Tourmaline ᕈ
> *"With love and joy, my heart is reborn."*

How Can I Use These Crystals for Attracting Love in My Life?

Display crystal word stones around your environment that have the word *Love* on them or any other words that represent aspects of love to you. You also can carry a love stone with you in your bag to take love with you wherever you go.

If you are dating, wear crystals such as rose quartz in a pendant or bracelet or put some in your pocket to help attract loving experiences. A small piece of black tourmaline can be helpful to protect against negative experiences. Aventurine is useful for good luck and keeping your heart chakra strong, and amethyst can calm your nerves and help you see clearly if a person or situation is right for you.

Keep pairs of crystals on your nightstand or one on each side of the bed to symbolize togetherness.

Choose a crystal to act as your love intention crystal, and program it with your intention. First, cleanse it. Then state your intention. Decide what you would like when it comes to love and put that into words. For example: "I love having a supportive, healthy, and committed partner in my life," or "I love knowing my ideal relationship is coming to me now," or "I am completely at home in a heart-and-soul-connected relationship." Hold on to your crystal and say your intention as often as you can, feeling it to be true and believing in its power.

When you meditate, **place a jade or emerald on your chest** to allow it to open your heart chakra to receive love.

On a full moon, go outside and hold a crystal, such as moonstone, carnelian, or watermelon tourmaline, and ask for assistance in releasing old emotional wounds and past hurts. Take a deep breath, and with your exhalation, imagine this hurt floating away, cleansing your system. You also can use a selenite wand to do the same, while moving it around your body and cutting the virtual cords that link to your past relationships. Make a swiping or cutting motion on each side of your body, front and back, above and below, saying with each one, "I release attachment to the past."

Crystal Activities for Attracting and Maintaining Love

1. Crystal Blind Dating

This is a fun activity to get you used to deciding what you would like and then receiving it in a lighthearted and playful way.

Write down traits that you would like in a crystal, but keep it to no more than five to ten to help you focus your intentions. For example, loving, understanding, honest, happy, positive, calming, beautiful, unique. Then take a few moments to feel the essence of these traits and how much you appreciate them. Next, go to a crystal store or browse online and choose one to three crystals that you feel embody some or all of these traits. Use your intuition rather than a directory of crystal properties. Feel the traits you have listed and then notice which crystals you feel drawn to. As your vibrational frequency is aligning with these traits, you will be attracting those crystals—and eventually those people and experiences—that can embody them. Take home your new crystals and put them in a special place, knowing that they represent your perfect match from an energetic perspective.

2. Displays of Love

This is like making an altar, but it involves making little love displays here and there, throughout your home, garden, and surroundings. You can have one special place to create a love attraction zone or altar, a bit like the one suggested in chapter 4, "Healthy Relationships," or you can create lots of displays so that you are symbolizing the presence of love everywhere in your life. Use crystals such as those suggested here or any others such as those you found via the crystal blind dating activity above. Place them in small groups alongside other items like flowers, candles, mementos, seashells, and motivational quote cards. Do a scan of your surroundings, think about where you can create love displays, and have fun with the process!

3. **Love Letters**
    Write two love letters: one to yourself and the other to your future partner. Healthy love starts with the self, so, first of all, while holding a rose quartz or rhodochrosite crystal, say everything you love about yourself and that you accept yourself no matter what. Tune in to your heart and the spiritual source of love that is you, and show your appreciation for the beautiful soul that you are. If needed, start out by recording a list of all the things you admire about yourself and then turn the list into a letter. Or, if you like, go straight into writing the letter. You may wish to display it somewhere you will see it regularly, such as beside your bed or stuck to your closet or bathroom mirror. Or simply put it in a special place.

    Now, write to your future partner, knowing and believing that they are out there somewhere and that you two will connect at the right time. You can hold the same crystals or your perfect match crystal from the blind dating activity. Tell them how much you are looking forward to meeting them, and describe what you love about them and all those unique little things that make them a special person in your life. Also, let them know you love them unconditionally and accept them as they are, and mention how being with them makes you feel. The more you can feel this as a reality, the easier it is to manifest this into your life. All manifestation is thought, vibration, and belief first, before you see it in your physical reality, so have fun with this and enjoy the positive anticipation. Keep the letter somewhere safe, and when you meet your partner who is the one you have written to, you may like to show it to them.

4. **Love Attraction Crystal Grid**
   Create a crystal grid using any or all the love crystals suggested here, either as a one-off for a love intention ritual or as something to keep on display. Enhance the effect by using a sacred geometry pattern as the base, or a preengraved wooden crystal grid, or print one from the Internet. Another idea is to print a mandala, fill it with your favorite colors, and use that as the base. When complete, state your love intention and any or all of the affirmations listed in this chapter to embody the manifesting power of the crystals.

5. **Use the affirmations listed for each crystal to help attract love, whether you have the crystal or not.**

6 FAMILY HARMONY

What Does Family Mean to Me?

Your family can be your biological family, adopted family, or friends. Whoever you see as your family, think about what having one means to you. What do you appreciate about it? How do they have a positive impact on your life and you on theirs? Do you like just knowing that someone is there for you, no matter what, or that you have a feeling of being bonded and supported in life? What do you love most about family?

There often can be family disharmony, due to different personalities and lifestyles. With those whom you would never walk away from and vice versa, learning ways to harmonize these connections is an important part of a happy life.

How Is Family Harmony Achieved?

Family harmony is achieved best when all members agree to make things work and support one another. When one or more members are not as agreeable, then an individual must learn ways to manage any conflict from their own perspective and stay in a space of love, forgiveness, and acceptance. When you focus on positive traits of those you love, despite any challenging issues, those negative concerns tend to lose their intensity. By being grateful more than being annoyed, you can help bring

about more harmony and peace. This is not to say that you put up with any unacceptable behaviors, but that you allow everyone to be human and make mistakes. Although you will stand up for yourself and what is right for you, you also will love them unconditionally.

Prioritizing time with your family to talk calmly through issues is a good way to get problems out into the open so that everyone is heard equally and next steps can be taken to resolve any conflict. It also can give everyone a chance to understand more about what another family member is going through or feeling, so you can have an opportunity to show compassion and support.

How Can Crystals Support Family Harmony?

Crystals can be a useful adjunct to other methods for enhancing family harmony. For a family who lives together, simply placing crystals around the home can help harmonize the living environment and support healthy communication and loving acceptance of one another. The high vibrations of crystals give off a healthy and harmonious energy that can have an impact on those in the environment.

You also can designate a crystal for the family to use as a "talking crystal" so that whenever you have a family discussion, the person who is talking can hold the crystal and know that they will be listened to. When they pass the crystal to the next person, then that person gets a chance to be heard as well. This is a great way to use crystals when it comes to family harmony, and holding the crystal and having an agreement around its use ensures that each person gets equal say in all matters.

Which Crystals Are Good for Supporting Harmony in My Family?

Each family member may have a crystal that resonates with them as an individual and helps them to be their best self. But there are certain crystals, such as sodalite, aquamarine, agate, and rose quartz, that you can use specifically when it comes to contributing to family harmony.

SODALITE

Sodalite is a blue-and-white-streaked crystal that is perfect for both the home environment and the family. Its main strength lies in its resonance with group dynamics and communication. It helps interactions to be harmonious and accepting and perception to be understanding and wise, and it allows individuals to speak with confidence and loving truth. It unites all in a clear and positive purpose, bringing a foundational strength to the family network and helping to keep the big picture relevant and front of mind so that you can avoid getting caught up in small issues that distract from a higher divine intent.

- Clearing and calming
- Harmony and belonging
- Understanding and acceptance
- Confident communication

> ☙ **Affirmation for Sodalite** ❧
> *"I communicate with love and respect*
> *for myself and my family."*

AQUAMARINE

This beautiful blue crystal with a green tinge has a smooth and clear appearance and nourishes the mind with calmness and clarity. It soothes and protects, reduces negativity, and helps you to see the light in the darkness. Aquamarine provides unclouded insight into life and allows you to communicate it to others, while bringing understanding and acceptance to all interactions. It benefits those who are highly sensitive, enhancing adaptation to surroundings and resilience of heart and mind, while protecting from excess stimulation and stress. Through its calming effect and encouragement of pure thought, it delivers confidence and courage and reduces feelings of regret and being overwhelmed. Aquamarine helps dispel built-up energy from the past, so you can move forward with peace.

- Confidence and courage
- Helps with speaking the truth
- Soothing and protective
- Releases judgment and blame

ॐ **Affirmation for Aquamarine** ॐ
*"I accept all that is and allow peace to
wash over me and my loved ones."*

AGATE

Agate crystals are popular for many uses, including jewelry and home decor, because of stunning patterns in their sliced form. But agate is also a strong healing stone that helps you find your inner strength, stability, and resilience and assists with understanding all the layers that make up our psychology, which allows us to act with love instead of fear. It is good for grounding, balance, and feeling supported in life. Agate crystals are helpful in situations where there have been emotional upheavals and where truth and soundness are needed.

Pink agate, in particular, can help with family harmony in relation to parenting, enhancing the bond between parent and child and deepening love and connection.

Green agate can aid with stabilizing disruptions and resolving conflict and assist with making decisions for the family so that all are satisfied.

Blue agate can reduce stress in the family and allow for calm communication, as well as strengthening bonds.

- Strength and stability
- Bond between parent and child
- Allowing love to dissolve fear
- Understanding and acceptance

❧ Affirmation for Agate ☙
"My family foundation is strong,
stable, loving, and calm."

ROSE QUARTZ

This light-pink crystal is easy to find and well-known for its gentle yet powerful vibration of love: love for the self, for life, and for others. It is suitable for all genders, yet embodies a feminine tenderness and caring energy that nurtures and supports. Rose quartz encourages unconditional love, bringing with it a sense of peace and acceptance. It reminds you to start with yourself, to embody the qualities of love, and to radiate this wherever you go so that others can feel the benefits of this, too, which helps them embody love. It also allows you to heal from past hurts and emotional difficulties, bringing clarity and knowledge that love always wins and is forever present in life. It will help to settle difficulties by enhancing the foundation of all harmony, which is love.

- Love of self and others
- Peace, acceptance, and harmony
- Emotional healing
- Dissolving of fear (the opposite of love)

❧ Affirmation for Rose Quartz ☙
"Love surrounds me and my loved ones
at all times."

How Can I Use These Crystals for Family Harmony?

Designate a crystal to be the family "talking crystal."

Decorate the dinner table with crystals, as part of a centerpiece and/or with one crystal for each place setting.

Add a key chain containing a crystal, such as a rose quartz, quartz, agate, or sodalite, to each set of keys for the family home.

Target your crystal choices to different rooms in the house, such as sodalite and agate for the kitchen and living room, amethyst and rose quartz for the bedrooms, quartz and aquamarine for the bathroom, and citrine and fluorite for the home office and study zones.

Wear crystal jewelry or carry stones in your pocket or bag when dealing with challenging people. For example, amazonite, tourmaline, sodalite, and rose quartz are good choices.

Give crystals as gifts to your family members. Use your intuition to choose ones that feels suited to them, or select ones based on their properties and purpose.

Crystal Activities for Family Harmony

1. **Family Time and the Talking Crystal**
    Designate some time each week or month as family discussion time. Set aside about thirty to sixty minutes, depending on the number of family members, where

each person gives a rundown of what they are up to and any issues or concerns they have about life or the family unit.

Use the "talking crystal" you have chosen, and allow each person to speak while holding this crystal. When everyone has had their say, you can then discuss anything that has to be resolved or make plans in the schedule so that everyone's needs are being honored.

2. Set the Table

Take all clutter off the family dining table, and make it a beautiful and harmonious space for meals and discussions. Create decorative place settings, and place a sodalite crystal next to each one as a symbol of unity within the household and to help with truthful and kind communication. You even may like to hide little notes of gratitude and inspiration under each place mat for a little dinnertime surprise. Create a centerpiece, as well, of fresh flowers or a decorative display of fruit or crystals in a bowl and a couple of candles.

3. Crystal Treasure Hunt

Here is a fun activity for families with children: hide a select number of crystals around the house or yard and then get the children to go on a treasure hunt. You may like to set a time limit for an extra challenge. Make a list of the crystals you have hidden and a fun fact about each one, so it is educational for them as well. When they find a crystal, let them try to figure out which one it is and then tick it off the list before going back to search for another one. This can be great for birthday parties too.

4. **Crystal Gratitude Box**

   A playful way to help family members focus on the positives in their life and within the family, thereby increasing overall harmony, is to have a small box or jar filled with a few crystals and a small notepad next to it to be used as a gratitude box. Get into the habit of writing down something good that happened each week or something learned or overcome. Fold the note up into a small bundle and place it in the box with the crystals. Keep doing this for a year, and at the end of it, read them all out loud and celebrate the blessings of you and your family. Then share the crystals, with each person getting one or two, and refill the box or jar with new crystals when the new year starts.

5. **Use the affirmations listed for each crystal to enhance family harmony as needed, whether you have the crystal or not.**

7 CREATING A SAFE HOME SANCTUARY

What Does "Home" Mean to Me?

"Home" means different things to different people, but in essence it is a place to feel safe and comfortable. For some, home is a feeling—a state of being at peace with wherever you are.

Home in the physical sense may be a house, an apartment, a tent, a caravan, a mansion, a room, a garden, or a hotel. Home can be portable or fixed, transient or permanent, so how you use crystals for the home will depend on your unique circumstances.

Before using crystals to enhance your home, think about what home means to you. What sort of environment is ideal for your lifestyle? How do you want to feel when you are at home?

Complete this sentence: "My ideal home feels . . ." (e.g., safe, comfortable, productive, harmonious, loving, private, vibrant, relaxing, etc.).

Imagine you are walking through the front door of your ideal home. What is the first thing you see? First thing you feel? First thing you do? What colors and scents are present? The more you can get a feeling of your ideal home, the easier it is to select appropriate crystals and apply other tips and tools to help create your safe and harmonious sanctuary.

How Can Crystals Enhance My Home Environment?

Because crystals have a naturally high vibration, they can have a positive impact on the energy or "feel" of the immediate environment and on people in the vicinity. Crystals in the home are beneficial for aesthetic and functional purposes: aesthetic in terms of adding color, texture, focal points, decoration, and symbolism; functional in terms of radiating specific energetic frequencies that can attune to and attract certain desired elements such as abundance, protection, love, and harmony. They can impact feelings, thoughts, and circumstances and allow the energy of your home to be high and clear. A home with good energy will feel clean, cozy, and welcoming and have a sense of flow in the surroundings.

Crystals can help enhance your sense of security and safety, your creativity and productivity, your health and happiness, your family dynamics, and your relationships. They can protect against electromagnetic radiation from home technology. They are also a wonderful talking point for visitors, making for positive and enlightening conversation.

Which Crystals Are Good for a Harmonious Home Life?

Answering the question about what home means to you will help determine which crystals are most beneficial and suited to you. However, there are some general options, including amazonite, selenite, tourmaline, quartz, and sodalite, that will benefit most people. You also can refer to the other chapters for crystals relating to health, relationships, family, and so forth, if certain topics are more relevant for your particular home life.

AMAZONITE

This beautiful greenish/aqua-colored crystal is a wonderful addition to the home because of its ability to act as a filter. It can sort out both physical and emotional negative energy, protect against electromagnetic radiation from home appliances such as microwaves, computers, televisions, and phones, and help prevent negative thoughts and emotions becoming dominant through its balancing action.

- Electromagnetic radiation protection
- Balances thoughts and emotions
- Hope and harmony
- Healthy communication

🔊 Affirmation for Amazonite 🔊
"My home is harmonious, clean, and protected."

SELENITE

This white, partly translucent crystal radiates a calm, clear light of peace. It is a gentle yet powerful link between the physical and the spiritual, allowing an anchoring of yourself into your surroundings while also strengthening your link to the energetic source of your being. It can moor your home to its surroundings, providing stability, but also connect it to a higher dimension of energy and power to protect and safeguard from negative influences in the external world.

- Security and protection
- Calm and peacefulness
- Divine guidance and wisdom
- Nurturing and cleansing

Power Point . . . Selenite should not get wet, or it may crumble or dissolve. So it is not a crystal to decorate your garden with, put into a medicinal elixir, or use in the bath!

> ⤳ Affirmation for Selenite ⤶
> *"My home is filled with only the energy*
> *I choose to allow and embrace."*

TOURMALINE

Like amazonite, tourmaline (the black variety is most common) is a useful crystal to have around the house to protect against radiation from electronic devices as well as negative emotional energy. It does this via its ability to transform energy, absorbing energy that is not beneficial and reforming it into a vibration that is more healthful. Because of its absorption ability, it benefits from regular cleansing so that it works more effectively. It also helps shield you from negative influences and can aid with any disharmony. Tourmaline is like a guardian of the home, the garden, and the self, creating a protective shield to maintain positive energy.

- Energy transformation
- Protector and guardian
- Provides a safe space for growth and nourishment
- Removes obstacles and blockages to well-being

> ❧ Affirmation for Tourmaline ❧
> *"I am safe and secure in*
> *my home and my body,*
> *and I thrive."*

QUARTZ

There are different types of quartz, but in this case, for the home, we are talking about clear quartz, which acts as a general energy amplifier and enhancer of the effects of other crystals, making it a helpful part of a crystal collection. Quartz is mostly transparent and comes in a variety of shapes and forms. It is the perfect crystal for when you do not know which crystal to use, because it will naturally tune in to your individual needs and provide what is necessary by strengthening the positive energy already present and dispersing any negativity. It has a calm and clear appearance and feel, making it a visually appealing crystal that suits all types of decor.

- Overall balancer and harmonizer
- Energy amplifier
- Cleansing and purifying
- Raises vibrations

Power Point . . . The benefits of quartz are not limited to the spiritual energy field. Science has discovered and is finding more ways that quartz can be used (for example, in watches and electronics).

౿ Affirmation for Quartz ⤇
*"My highest self is ever-present and active,
and my surroundings reflect my calm
and clear energy."*

SODALITE

Sodalite is a blue-and-white-streaked crystal that is perfect for both the physical aspects of home environment and the relationship dynamics within it. It can be used for electromagnetic protection from computers and phones, but its main strength lies in its resonance with group dynamics and communication. It helps interactions to be harmonious and accepting and perception to be understanding and wise, and it allows individuals to speak with confidence and loving truth. It unites all in a clear and positive purpose, helping to keep the big picture relevant and front of mind so that you can avoid getting caught up in small issues that distract from a higher divine intent.

- Clearing and calming
- Harmony and teamwork
- Understanding and acceptance
- Confident communication

To help you fully embrace the power of sodalite for the home, read this message as though it is coming from a wise friend.

Dear Confident One,

You have all the wisdom and ability within you to maintain harmony in your home and life. You need not be afraid of expressing your true self or being who you are. Find that sense of home inside you, and you will always feel comfortable and confident in speaking your truth. Your loving words have immense power to heal and harmonize, and when you come from a place of love and trust, you can dispel conflict and ease challenges. Carry me with you when you need a physical reminder of your inner power, and meditate with me to access your inner wisdom and insights, which can then help others. Remember everyone's unique perspectives and value each person for the gifts they bring to life. Accept and embrace diversity of views, beliefs, and communication styles. Enjoy the peace and harmony that is available to you with your confident communication.

Love,

Sodalite

≈ Affirmation for Sodalite ≈
*"My communication is loving and truthful,
and so is that of those around me."*

How Can I Use These Crystals in the Home?

Crystal grids for general or varied purposes are a visually appealing and powerful addition to any home. Create an overall "home" grid using the crystals mentioned in this chapter, and place it near the entrance of your house or in the main living area. (See "Crystal Grids" on pages 21–22.) You also can create grids for relationship harmony, family well-being, health and happiness, and abundance and prosperity, and you can even make one in your garden with crystals suitable for use in the outdoors, along with flowers, plants, shells, and other stones. Grids can be placed on tables, shelves, plates, and trays, or you can produce a piece of art with crystal grid photographs and display it on a wall.

Place selenite crystals in each corner of your home to create a protective frame that filters and decides what does and does not enter. This will help anchor your home to harmonize with its surroundings, while connecting it to divine energetic protection. You also can use selenite lamps or Himalayan salt lamps to add a healing and protective touch to your home.

Put black tourmaline in the garden to protect plants and encourage growth, either placed around the plants or buried in the soil. Try putting some small pieces in a vegetable patch or herb garden, and visualize the plants growing and providing healthy nourishment.

Use crystals as a form of home decor, basing your decorating around the colors of the crystals. For example, use aqua and light-green colors and lots of light tones like white and soft pastels with amazonite crystals to create a harmonious nature-themed living room. Add the following companions to enhance the beauty and effect of the crystals: flowers, plants, essential oil diffusers, candles, shells, word stones, books, and art.

Household electromagnetic radiation protection: keep amazonite next to your phone (especially if you keep it in your pocket) and phone charger, or wear amazonite earrings to act as a filter between your phone and your ear. Use amazonite refrigerator magnets and crystals placed next to computers, televisions, and microwaves. Sodalite also can be used in this way.

Place a black tourmaline inside or outside the front door to act as a guard for your home.

Add a variety of quartz crystals to each room in your home. They can be placed next to candles, taped to a door, incorporated into wind chimes or mobiles, or used in crystal grids.

Crystal Activities for Creating Your Safe Home Sanctuary

1. **Home Assessment and Home Enhancement**
    Walk around your home and make a list of any areas that feel out of balance or uncomfortable or that have a lot of manmade materials or technology. Jot down how you want these areas to feel instead, then choose appropriate crystals and ways to use them to enhance the energy of that particular area. For example: *My bedroom feels messy*

and overstimulating. I want it to feel relaxed and sensual.
I will remove excess clutter and electronic devices, and use
amazonite and rose quartz to balance and provide a loving
and peaceful environment.

2. **Finding a New Home**

    When searching for a new place to reside, choose a crystal,
    such as clear quartz or any that you feel drawn to that
    brings you a feeling of "home" and comfort, and program
    it to help attract this ideal place. First, cleanse your crystal
    in full sunlight or moonlight for a few hours. Then hold the
    crystal and meditate with it, while visualizing and feeling
    what home means to you, and ask it to help you find the
    right dwelling. Every time you look at a potential home,
    bring the crystal with you, hold it as you walk around, and
    become aware of any extra warmth or sensation in it as it
    interprets the surroundings. Use your intuition, enhanced by
    the crystal, to help guide your decision-making.

3. **Housewarming/Homewarming**

    If you are moving into a new place, before putting all your
    belongings into it, start by smudging the space with sage or
    using a sage spray. You can buy sage herb smudging sticks
    and abalone shells, which you can use to catch any burned
    herb and help disperse the smoke. As you waft the smoke
    around the rooms, ask spirit to cleanse the premises of any
    negative energy from previous occupants and state that
    you will fill the home with love, positivity, and peace.

Alternatively, spray each corner with sage spray or crystal cleansing spray. Then spray toward the ceiling and the ground and in the middle of each room, visualizing all the stored negative energy to be removed and cleared, ready for your new positive energy. Add your selenite crystals to each corner, and begin making your new house a home.

4. **Create a Home Crystal Grid**

Using the guidance at the start of the book on pages 21–22, create a permanent crystal grid to display somewhere in your home with the crystals recommended in this chapter and/or specific crystals for areas you want to maximize, such as love, communication, and health. You could place it as a centerpiece on your dining table, in the entryway on a table, or in the living room on a side table or coffee table. You also can take a photograph of your grid and have it printed and framed.

5. **Home Photo Board**

A home photo board is a bit like a vision board. Use a piece of cardboard or a pinboard to make a collage of photos and images and words that represent happy home memories, home goals, and the positive feelings you want in your home. Add photos of crystals, or stick small crystals on it. If you are using a pinboard, stick a pin through the hook on crystal jewelry pendants.

6. **Create an "At Home" Ritual**
   Anytime you need to feel grounded, secure, safe, or protected, create and utilize a self-guided "at home" ritual, like a personalized meditation, that will help anchor you to your home and enhance your feelings of it. Choose one or two crystals that you associate with home, hold one or both in your hands, close your eyes, and feel your connection to your home—through your feet and your other senses—and imagine a protective white light around you. Repeat an affirmation that feels right to you, such as those suggested for each crystal in this chapter or one of your own. For example: "I am completely free to be me, and I am comfortable and safe right now" or "I carry the feeling of home with me no matter where I am in the world." Place your hand on a wall, take a deep breath, and feel its strength and support.

7. **Use the affirmations listed for each crystal, whether you have the crystal or not.**

8 WORKPLACE HARMONY, CAREER DREAMS, AND LIFELONG LEARNING

The Importance of Workplace Harmony, Career Dreams, and Lifelong Learning

Harmony in the workplace is often a battle for many people in a variety of professions. Naturally, there are going to be differing personalities and beliefs and different ways of doing things, and many challenges and conflicts occur when under pressure. Disharmony can result from a number of things: being overworked; being underrecognized; being criticized; not being listened to; not having enough time to complete a task; or when pressure and demands escalate, a person under stress affects others as well.

Restoring workplace harmony is possible and is an important part of job satisfaction and productivity. It requires comprehensive strategies and the cooperation of all, but there are things you can do for yourself to impact the vibration you are giving off, making you more likely to attract good experiences and interactions.

When you think about your job, what comes to mind? Are you doing it for money only, or are you passionate about your career and how you can achieve more within your field? When you feel passion for your career and excitement about future possibilities, anything is possible if you believe and take initiative.

The same goes for study and learning. It is a way of becoming highly skilled or knowledgeable about a topic, which may lead to a new career or enhance the one you have got. And life itself is an ongoing learning experience. Whether you are doing an official learning program of some kind or just reading and experiencing life and learning things here and there, the thirst for knowledge is part of being human. The more desire you have to learn new things, the more purpose you have and the easier it can be to keep motivated and enjoy your life. Learning encourages new neural pathways in the brain, helping you retain information but also associating it with different contexts and integrating it into your life.

How Can Crystals Enhance My Workplace, Career, and Learning?

Crystals are a great tool for the workplace because you do not have to have everyone on board for them to work! When you use them, you may find people actually become more communicative and agreeable because when people feel good and are happy and comfortable in their work environment, surrounded by positive things, it naturally flows out into their daily interactions and duties.

Crystals can emit a subtle and harmonious vibration that impacts those around them. They look nice as a decoration, too, and most workplaces do try to enhance the visual appeal of the workspace to make it comfortable for employees to do their job. So crystals are an easy form of decor in addition to the usual items like flowers, paintings, and sculptures.

Crystals also help with learning because they are a great way to harness concentration and memory. Use them as both an object of focus for learning and memorizing and a high-vibration energy transmitter to assist with study demands and with focusing your intentions for your career dreams.

Which Crystals Are Good for the Workplace, Career, and Learning?

Focus on crystals that have properties which enhance stability, concentration, communication, protection, harmony, abundance, and clarity.

Eight crystals that help in this regard are red jasper, sodalite, onyx, fluorite, pyrite, amazonite, aquamarine, and mahogany obsidian.

RED JASPER

This earthy-red crystal is a solid-looking stone with properties that enhance the feeling of stability and security, which is helpful in the workplace if job security is not guaranteed. All jasper crystals

have a grounding effect and nurture the body while stabilizing the emotions. Red jasper is helpful when you feel that you have to do everything on your own, bringing you a sense of belonging and connectedness and helping you to see the unity of all people and your place and value in the world. It will bring strength during times of hardship and fluctuating emotions or in environments of unpredictability, allowing a natural balance to occur and settling overactive responses. With its stabilizing effects, it supports endurance and the ability to keep going and to withstand the effects of chronic stress and brings forth a consistency of determination and strength.

- Grounding and security
- Stabilizes the emotions
- Supports feelings of belonging and connection
- Balancing and settling effects

⇗ Affirmation for Red Jasper ⇖
"I am stable and grounded within my workplace, happily connected to the collective purpose we share together."

SODALITE

Sodalite is a blue-and-white-streaked crystal that is perfect for both the physical aspects of the work environment and the relationship dynamics within the workplace. It can be used for electromagnetic protection from computers and phones, but its main strength lies in its resonance with group dynamics and communication. It helps interactions to be harmonious and accepting and perception to be understanding and wise, and it allows individuals to speak with confidence and loving truth. It unites all in a clear and positive purpose, helping to keep the big picture relevant and front of mind so that you can avoid getting caught up in small issues that distract from a higher divine intent. It is also helpful for individuals, allowing for authenticity and truthfulness with themselves and others and stimulating productivity and efficiency.

- Clearing and calming
- Harmony and teamwork
- Understanding and acceptance
- Confident communication

☙ Affirmation for Sodalite ❧
*"My communication is truthful and authentic,
and I am calm and productive at work."*

ONYX

Onyx is a black stone, sometimes with a few small white or gray patches or bands. It is not as glassy in appearance compared to obsidian, which can help distinguish the two. Onyx makes you feel strong and stable wherever you go, protecting you from sudden changes or negative influences in your surroundings, and can therefore be helpful for difficult or stressful work situations. It is also beneficial for those who are sensitive and need to feel comfortable and safe within themselves. It assists with endurance and getting through challenges and long work hours, while creating a balance of energies around you.

- ☀ Protection and security
- ☀ Strength and endurance
- ☀ Stress relief
- ☀ Balancing and stabilizing

❧ Affirmation for Onyx ☙
"I am strong within myself and protected at all times."

FLUORITE

Fluorite is available in different colors such as blue, purple, green, and clear, and rainbow fluorite, which is a combination of these colors, is very popular. Fluorite is the crystal for focus and organization. It aids concentration, processing of information, organizing of thoughts, and retention of relevant information. It also helps to minimize distractions and negative influences, including from technology, so that the brain can function at its best and the mind can be clear and calm. It allows you to assimilate information from both mental and spiritual realms so that you can contextualize what you are learning in a broader sense and give depth and understanding of a topic. Fluorite helps you put your thoughts into a clear structure and make sense of them as a whole, while helping you work as part of a team with harmony.

- ☀ Focus and concentration
- ☀ Processing and assimilation of information
- ☀ Reduces negative influences and electromagnetic radiation
- ☀ Teamwork and purpose

༄ **Affirmation for Fluorite** ༄
*"I am focused and organized at work,
and so are those around me."*

PYRITE

You only need to look at this opulent gold crystal (also known as "fool's gold") to know it is something special. It naturally holds and radiates abundant energy and draws it in. It encourages feelings of confidence and worthiness to allow you to achieve your goals and accomplish tasks. It is helpful to use in the workplace to enhance abundance and success, and during study for concentration and memory, while assisting in keeping out negative influences.

- ❀ Success magnet
- ❀ Energy magnifier
- ❀ Confidence and worthiness
- ❀ Productivity and concentration

❧ Affirmation for Pyrite ☙
"I am aligned with the vibration of success."

AMAZONITE

This beautiful greenish/aqua-colored crystal is wonderful for releasing negative emotions and vibrations in the environment because of its ability to act as a filter. It can sort out both physical and emotional negative energy, protect against electromagnetic radiation from office appliances and technology, and help to prevent negative thoughts and emotions becoming dominant through its balancing action. It helps to harmonize communication and interactions through its ability to shift vibrations to the positive side and bring clarity from all perspectives, having a regulating effect on people in the surrounding area. It is a stone of hope, allowing bright possibilities to be illuminated and pursued.

- Protection from negative frequencies
- Balances thoughts and emotions
- Hope and harmony
- Healthy communication

❧ Affirmation for Amazonite ☙
"My workplace is harmonious and healthy."

AQUAMARINE

This beautiful blue crystal with a green tinge has a smooth and clear appearance, and it nourishes the mind with calmness and clarity. It soothes and protects, reduces negativity, and helps you to see the light in the darkness. Aquamarine provides unclouded insight into life and allows you to communicate it to others, while bringing understanding and acceptance to all interactions. It benefits those who are highly sensitive, enhancing adaptation to surroundings and resilience of heart and mind, while protecting from excess stimulation and stress. Through its calming effect and encouragement of pure thought, it brings confidence and courage and reduces feelings of regret and being overwhelmed. Aquamarine helps dispel built-up energy from the past, so you can move forward with peace.

- Confidence and courage
- Helps with speaking the truth
- Soothing and protective
- Releases judgment and blame

༖ **Affirmation for Aquamarine** ༝
*"I accept all that is and allow peace and calm
to flow into my workplace."*

MAHOGANY OBSIDIAN

Mahogany obsidian is a reddish-brown-colored crystal with black flecks, and it gives a double action: grounding/stability and protection from negativity. It resonates with the earth frequencies and brings certainty to the surface, helping with feelings of security and safety. Its protective properties help filter out unnecessary negative influences and keep you focused on positive aspects. This crystal is useful for gaining clarity about your dreams and goals, bringing a sense of purpose, and assisting with making decisions about your future.

- Clear decisions
- Purpose and determination
- Safety and security
- Protection and positivity

> ☙ Affirmation for Mahogany Obsidian ❧
> *"The decisions I make are always right for me."*

How Can I Use These Crystals for My Job, Career, and Learning?

If you have a job that involves a lot of multitasking and spur-of-the-moment demands, you may feel ungrounded and scattered, so try carrying a red jasper with you or wearing a red jasper bracelet or anklet to help keep you feeling grounded and stable.

If you have to give a presentation, wear a sodalite pendant or earrings to help you speak clearly and express yourself effectively.

If you have to work around negative people or those who complain a lot, bring onyx with you to work and keep it close. Another option is tourmaline, either black or watermelon tourmaline, to help filter out the negativity and keep you heart-focused and able to communicate without getting worked-up or defensive.

Keep a piece of fluorite on your desk to help you focus on your tasks.

Place some amazonite near computers, printers, and other technology to harmonize the energy.

Keep some aquamarine handy for your breaks to help you momentarily switch off from work or study and enjoy some peace and calm.

Hold a mahogany obsidian crystal whenever you need to make important decisions.

Bring an aventurine with you to job interviews, business meetings, conference calls, or conferences.

When sitting for exams or doing workplace training, bring a "good luck," "calming," or "focus" crystal in your pocket or wear one as jewelry. A ring on your finger can be a good option if you are doing a handwritten exam, or a pendant if you need to feel calm and centered.

When doing rote memory learning, hold a crystal as you recite what it is you have to remember. The action of holding a specific object will help your brain associate it with the words or information you need to memorize.

Choose a crystal, such as citrine, for career or abundance to attach to your car keys, house keys, or office keys.

Crystal Activities for Workplace Harmony, Career Dreams, and Lifelong Learning

1. Positive Traits List

Write a list of all the main people you work alongside, and next to their names jot down at least one, but preferably three or more, positive traits or observations about them. Even if you find them negative or difficult to work with, find something to appreciate. Any time you deal with them and have any challenging situations, keep in mind the positive traits you wrote down. Even better, if the opportunity arises, tell them what you appreciate about them. When it suits the moment, just make a comment such as "Hey, Lucy, I really admire how quickly you work through those documents" or "You're so nice to customers on the phone. You have a really friendly nature."

When you have recorded your list (include yourself on it), go through it one person at a time and intuitively think of a crystal for them. You do not have to give them one (although you could); just decide which one feels right for them. If you do not know many crystals yet, flip through this book and see what you are drawn to. Write down the crystal name next to them, and energetically bless them with their properties, through your genuine intention.

2. Decision-Making Process

Write down a list of decisions you need to make for your career or questions you would like answers to or options to consider. Use a mahogany obsidian crystal to help you get clarity. Set an intention for the crystal to help you, by holding it and asking it to serve the purpose of assisting in your decision-making for the highest good of yourself and all involved.

Go through the questions one at a time, perhaps starting with a less important decision. While holding the crystal, close your eyes and take a few deep breaths, tuning into that part of you that knows intuitively what is right. Either in your mind or out loud, ask your question. Ask succinctly and directly, without urgency or need, just a calm and simple question. Notice the first feeling or thought that comes to you, before your logical mind kicks in. You may wish to jot down any key words or answers, and be sure to listen for the answer before jumping in and analyzing it or judging it. Let it show itself. If it does not or it is not clear enough, go to a different question and come back to that one later.

Anytime you have a decision to make, trust your intuition and your own insight, and use the crystal as an extra guide to assist in this process.

3. Positivity Zone

If possible, make a staff positivity zone or table, with crystals, flowers, cups of tea, treats, and a jar with bits of paper next to it for people to write down positive things that happened at work or things they appreciate about staff members (anonymously, if they wish). At regular intervals or at staff meetings, empty the jar and read all the notes out loud. You can even have the person with the most positive statements get a reward of some kind. If all workplaces tried this, harmony and job satisfaction would be enhanced greatly. It encourages people to focus on something good each day and document it, adding to the healthy vibes.

4. Team Meetings

As suggested in the "Family Harmony" chapter, if your workplace has regular team meetings, consider having a "talking crystal" that each person holds while speaking before passing it to the next person. This will allow them to be heard fully and not interrupted so that they may express anything that is on their minds and get equal say.

And if you do not have team meetings, why not start? They need only be a brief check-in with everyone to make sure everyone's concerns are addressed and rapport can be established.

5. Career Vision Board

Even if you have already made a vision board, making one specifically for your career is a super fun way to charge up your work life. A career vision board can help you clarify what it is you love about your job or the career you want, and the feelings it brings you. Once you know what career means to you and what your goals and dreams are, bring them to life in picture form on a big piece of paper or cardboard, a corkboard, a whiteboard, or a bulletin board.

When you are going through any challenges, keeping an eye on your vision board helps to keep you focused on what really matters and to stay positive about the future.

Decide on your background for the board. If you want to change up the images on a regular basis to adjust your course as you go, then a corkboard or bulletin board is a good idea. But there is also power in using cardboard and glue, because gluing pictures on is a symbol of commitment and certainty and putting faith in your visions to manifest.

Flip through magazines and brochures and search the Internet for photos to cut out and stick on, as well as words and phrases that match your career dreams. Do not worry about whether something seems unrealistic or not achievable. If you are drawn to it and it feels good to look at or think about, then use it. The images will, of course, depend on your chosen career, but some also may be generic, like smiling faces of people you work with, handshakes to symbolize agreements, financial-related rewards, travel, and whatever symbolizes being happy and successful. Do not only focus on physical and material images; also use pictures that are more abstract or have a good "feeling" about them. Think of it not just as a vision board but also as a *feeling* board.

When you have got all your images and words, play around with the arrangement. You also can add stickers or other decorations, and real crystals in small chips or flat pieces that are not too heavy, or print out photos of crystals that you want to associate with your career.

Place your board somewhere you will see it often, and smile and enjoy the feeling of unlimited possibilities!

6. **Crystal Grid for Career Enhancement**

If you would like to enhance your current job or improve your chances for a promotion or opportunity, try making a crystal grid for that area of your life. See pages 21–22 for full details on making crystal grids, but in general, choose a backing surface or a round item like a plate or board and arrange crystals in a circular geometric pattern, radiating out from the center. Use any of the crystals suggested in this chapter and/ or those that relate specifically to your job goals. You also can add anything else that symbolizes success, such as coins if you are wanting more income, or smiley face stickers if you are desiring more enjoyment. Craft specific intentions such as "I am so grateful to receive an unexpected bonus" or one overall intention such as "I love and enjoy my job."

When your grid is complete, for it to do its magic, hold your hands over the grid and state your intention out loud, taking a few deep breaths and imagining your intention being absorbed into the crystals and directed upward through the center and out into the universe.

7. **Complementary Tools to Use with These Crystals**

Play music in the background while you work or study. Classical music such as Mozart is best and is well known to enhance concentration and memory.

Diffuse essential oils, or use them as a skin cream or ointment on your temples. Lemon, rosemary, peppermint, and ylang-ylang are particularly helpful.

Stay hydrated, so the brain can function at its best. Sip water every fifteen minutes.

Do regular movement and stretching to keep blood flowing healthily through the body and to allow neck and shoulder muscles to relax.

Rest periodically, even for a few minutes, to allow for consolidation of knowledge and for the brain to recover in between stimulating activities.

Keep a plant or flowers near your workstation to bring some nature and oxygen into your environment.

8. **Use the affirmations listed for each crystal whenever you need more workplace harmony or help with your career dreams or learning, whether you have the crystal or not.**

9 FERTILITY AND PREGNANCY

The Gift of Creating Life

Pregnancy and parenthood are two of life's most amazing experiences. The gift of life is not only about bringing a new human being into the world, it is also a time of nourishment, growth, transformation, and rebirth for the parents. For the mother, it is often a time of awareness and amazement at the human body and awakening to her inner strength and nature as a woman.

A number of women achieve pregnancy easily and quickly; for some it is unplanned; and for others it can take a bit longer or even years of trying through natural means or medical intervention. And for some people it never eventuates, or they may become parents in another way. Regardless, it is one of the most important times for nourishing the self and making physical and mental health a top priority. The gift of life is a blessing and one of the most special times in a person's life.

How Can Crystals Enhance My Fertility and Help with a Healthy Pregnancy?

Just as crystals begin as energy and natural materials forming together to create something unique, so does a baby. It is often seen as a purely physical experience, but for those who understand and embrace the energetic nature of all things, life always begins with energy. Crystals, with their energetic properties, can be wonderful adjuncts to this physical process by helping the parents, and the mother in particular, start with a strong and high energetic foundation. Using crystals throughout pregnancy can then help with maintaining this high vibration and assist the mother who has emotional and physical discomfort or concerns to keep things in balance.

Which Crystals Are Good for Fertility and Pregnancy?

There are particular crystals whose frequencies relate more strongly to fertility and pregnancy. For fertility, men and women can use them equally, though some will relate more to one than to the other. For pregnancy, crystals can help not only the mother but also her partner.

Crystals that are especially helpful for maximizing fertility and sustaining a healthy pregnancy include moonstone, rose quartz, garnet, selenite, mookaite, unakite, and pink agate.

MOONSTONE

We all know the powerful effect the moon has on the Earth, and it is the same with our bodies, through water and energy. The moonstone crystal is a way to harness this moon energy more directly, as it balances the ebb and flow of our emotions and the natural cycles of life, such as with fertility and reproduction. Moonstone can help you feel connected, supported, and in the flow of life, allowing you to surrender and receive natural blessings in perfect divine timing.

- Fertility booster
- Balance
- Unity and connection
- Enhances feminine energy

Power Point . . . Natural moonstone has a peachy, grayish color, whereas rainbow moonstone is a variation of labradorite and has a luminescent white-gray appearance with a subtle blue glow.

> ❧ Affirmation for Moonstone ❧
> *"I flow with the natural cycles of life and welcome healing moon energy into all my cells."*

ROSE QUARTZ

This light-pink crystal is easy to find and well-known for its gentle yet powerful vibration of love—love for the self, for life, and for others. It is suitable for all genders, yet embodies a feminine tenderness and caring energy that nurtures and supports. Rose quartz encourages unconditional love, bringing with it a sense of peace and acceptance. It reminds you to start with yourself, to embody the qualities of love, and to radiate this wherever you go. It also allows you to heal from past hurts and emotional difficulties, bringing clarity and knowledge that love always wins and is forever present in life.

- Love of self and others
- Peace and acceptance
- Emotional healing
- Dissolving of fear (the opposite of love)

GARNET

Most often used is the deep reddish-black crystal known for its warming and nourishing effects that allow the body to rejuvenate and regain passion. It can assist with adding dynamic energy to reproductive power and aiding in fertility issues associated with high stress levels or lack of desire. It encourages dedication between couples, strengthening the bond to enhance fertility and conception.

- Energy booster
- Enhances connection, desire, and bonding
- Strengthening
- Self-confidence and personal power

SELENITE

This white, partly translucent crystal has a calm, clean radiance. It gently cleanses the surrounding areas, including negative energy buildup in the environment and the body, making it useful for the home and bedroom. Through its purifying effect, it can help with reducing the harmful impact of technology and chemicals, rendering it a good crystal to use alongside others for fertility and pregnancy to support a low-toxicity lifestyle and help clear any energy that is disrupting reproductive power. It also helps connect to divine energy, calling in your unborn child with its pure and calming energy.

- Support and protection for a strong foundation in the body and home
- Calm and peaceful energy
- Divine connection and communication
- Nurturing and cleansing

⮞ Affirmation for Selenite ⮜
"My mind and body are clean, calm, and safe."

MOOKAITE

Also known as "Australian jasper," this beautiful stone with smooth, curving color combinations of earthy-red, orangey-yellow, and brown resembles the Australian outback landscape. It is filled with strong earth energy, while also being a link to past and future. It is said to be a useful crystal for communicating with the spirits of unborn children and connecting with their energy as you start on your fertility or pregnancy journey. Mookaite is valuable for wound healing and immune system health, for regenerating cells and tissues, and for postnatal recovery.

- ❋ Physical health and recovery
- ❋ Spirit communication
- ❋ Adaptability to changing circumstances
- ❋ Link between physical and spiritual, past and future

☙ **Affirmation for Mookaite** ❧
"I enjoy good health in mind, body, and spirit."

UNAKITE

Easily recognizable by its contrasting green and orangey-pink patches, this crystal is a great choice for supporting overall health in pregnancy as well as transforming negative buildup from the past into the present, so it can be released and removed. It helps prospective parents to release past wounds so that they need not be carried on to future generations.

Unakite also can help support the body when physical conditions are affecting the reproductive organs and encourage new cell growth and development. In addition, it is a strong link between the physical and spiritual, assisting with psychic experiences.

- ❋ Support for physical health and healing
- ❋ Reproductive and pregnancy health
- ❋ Psychic enhancement
- ❋ Releasing the past

⊱ Affirmation for Unakite ⊰
*"I am strong and balanced and
ready to nourish new life."*

PINK AGATE

Agate crystals are popular for many uses, including jewelry and home decor, because of their stunning patterns in sliced form. Agate is also a strong healing stone that helps you find your inner strength and stability and your resilience, and it assists with understanding all the layers that make up our psychology, allowing us to act with love instead of fear. It is good for grounding, balance, and feeling supported in life. Pink agate, in particular, is associated with parent-and-child bonding and deepening love and connection.

- Strength and stability
- Bond between parent and child
- Allowing love to dissolve fear
- Understanding and acceptance

⊱ Affirmation for Pink Agate ⊰
*"I am lovingly connected to divine energy
and to my child."*

How Can I Use These Crystals for My Fertility and Pregnancy?

Keep them close to you, in pockets, or wear as jewelry.

Hold your chosen crystal in your hand each morning, and repeat an affirmation or intention relating to your baby goals.

Get selenite lamps for your bedside tables to keep the air clean and fresh and to protect from environmental and emotional stress. These are also good for the delivery room.

Place a few of these crystals on body parts (such as over your abdomen where your ovaries and uterus are) during meditation and visualization. If you meditate with your partner, each of you also can place a crystal over your heart to amplify love and connection.

Place garnet beside the bed for stimulating sexual energy.

Communicate with the unborn child with the assistance of mookaite and moonstone or selenite. Hold the crystal, and meditate with it. Then gently tell your baby you are here and lovingly awaiting their arrival and anything else you would like to communicate to them. Do not be surprised if you feel the crystal getting warmer or starting to pulse or vibrate.

Have rose quartz baths during pregnancy to nourish yourself and the baby with unconditional love.

Massage sore muscles with a smooth, rounded crystal of medium size, or ask your partner or someone else to assist. Unakite or mookaite can be a good option for this.

Create a birthing kit with crystals to place under the bed, on the bedside, and in other areas of the birthing room, and a piece of jewelry to wear during birth. Use any of the crystals mentioned here, particularly selenite, rose quartz, and pink agate, and for after the birth, unakite and mookaite for healing, and moonstone to connect you to divine feminine and mothering energy and give gratitude for your precious gift.

Crystal Activities for Fertility and Pregnancy

1. **Full Moon Ritual with Moonstone**
    Supercharge your crystals, especially moonstone, under a full moon by placing them outside overnight (except selenite, if it may get wet or damp) to absorb more direct moon energy. You also can simply hold them in your hands on the night of the full moon and state an intention you wish to program into your crystals, such as "Thank you, universe, for the power of the moon and of this crystal. I ask that this crystal be infused with healing energy and the intention of receiving a healthy pregnancy and baby."
    Do this separately with each crystal or all of them together. When leaving your crystals out overnight, place them on a tray, on a table, or on the earth. If you have any tree stumps around, they are also great for charging crystals on or making a crystal grid with, because they are

exposed to the energy of growth and strength from the tree
as well.

2. Fertility Meditation

Carve out regular time in your schedule for a relaxing
crystal meditation to center yourself and connect with your
feminine energy and the magnificence of your body and
reproductive organs. For this meditation, you will need
one garnet crystal, two moonstones (both the same type, or
one natural and one rainbow), and one or two rose quartz.
Prepare a space where you can comfortably lie down on
your back (in the bed or space where your baby is most
likely to be conceived), and place the garnet on the sacral
chakra area on your lower abdomen/pubic region, the rose
quartz on the area above your uterus, and one moonstone
on the area above each ovary. You also may place a rose
quartz on your chest to connect your heart and womb
with the energy of love. You can be fully clothed for this
or naked, if you have a light sheet or blanket to cover you
because you may get cold while you are relaxed and your
breathing slows down.

When the crystals are in place, position your arms by
your side with palms facing upward in receiving mode,
close your eyes, and take as many deep, slow breaths as
needed to feel relaxed and calmly aware of your body.
Imagine the energy of the crystals warming and nourishing
your reproductive area, then focus on one crystal at a time.
Starting with the garnet on your lower abdomen/pubic

region, take a deep breath and imagine your inhalation drawing in the warming energy of the garnet. Visualize rich, red, nourishing energy filling your sacral chakra and reproductive organs with life-giving boosts of energy. Feel gratitude for the opportunity to conceive and to either have a partner to share this with or a medical option to assist you. Feel gratitude for all the life-force energy available to you. Say in your mind, "Thank you for the opportunity to conceive."

Next, focus on the moonstones on your ovary areas and feel the moon energy entering your ovaries with your inhalation. Experience it as a gentle pulse, allowing the healing energy of the universe to nourish these organs and assist in their cycles, in egg health, and in the ovulation process. Visualize an egg releasing easily and finding its way into the fallopian tube. Say, "Thank you for an easy and timely ovulation."

Now, move your awareness to the rose quartz above your uterus. Breathe in, and feel the love flooding your entire uterus and radiating out to all your reproductive organs and whole body and the room around you. Visualize the moment of conception: a sperm meeting the egg and connecting, uniting, merging. Sense the joy of this miraculous process. Imagine how it will be when you receive a positive pregnancy test. Say, "Thank you for a healthy conception and pregnancy."

Now that your reproductive areas are filled with loving and nourishing crystal energy, focus your awareness on

your heart and fill it with emotions of love and gratitude.
Smile softly. Dwell on this beautiful feeling for as long
as you wish, and open your eyes when ready. Return to
this meditation often to help you stay in receiving mode,
allowing a healthy conception into your life.

3. **Create a Fertility Bracelet**
   Purchase or make your own bracelet, using the crystals
   mentioned in this chapter, plus any others you feel drawn
   to or good all-rounders like carnelian, amethyst, and
   tourmaline for releasing negative thoughts or fears around
   conceiving. These can be bought or made using either
   crystal chips, which have more jagged, rough edges, or
   smooth polished stones that may be round or oval. Rose
   quartz and moonstone is a great basic combination. You
   also can create a birthing bracelet with the crystals you
   want to use to help you in childbirth, although if having
   a Cesarean section, you may not be able to wear jewelry,
   so simply wear it after the delivery. Make sure you use
   smooth tumbled stones for the birth process so that when
   your baby is born you do not risk hurting their fragile skin
   with the crystal chips.

   There are many jewelry-making resources and
   materials online. All you may need is some fishing line or
   an elastic string to thread crystals with predrilled holes.
   Then tie the ends together or attach a jewelry clasp. You
   also could ask a jewelry maker to make one for you or find
   one that has been premade. Before wearing it, cleanse it in

the sunlight or under moonlight, preferably a full moon, for a few hours.

4. **Life Creation Vision Book**

    Immerse yourself in the joy and gift of life in all forms by creating a vision book. Just like a vision board, it is a collage of images and words, except you can keep adding to it and include a lot more pictures. Find a journal or notebook or a visual art diary with good-quality paper, preferably spiral bound, so you can lay it flat when working with crystals and intentions. Fill it with pictures from magazines, catalogs, brochures, or old greeting cards, or use hand-drawn ones. Choose images that represent new life to you. You can be more literal by including images of babies, pregnant bellies, couples in love, passionate embraces, baby clothes; images of baby animals like ducklings, puppies, and kittens; and flowers that are starting to bloom or have just blossomed. They also can be more "feeling based," which simply evoke emotions that are nourishing and supporting and make you feel open to receiving and being blessed with extraordinary gifts. Use any pictures that make you feel good, that represent new life and growth and love, and that fill you with love and connection and blessedness. You can use words and phrases, too, or write your own. Each page can be a combination of different images or of one theme. It is up to you. Have fun with the process! It is even more powerful if partners do this together, each choosing a selection of images and words and then putting them together.

To add the energy of crystals to your vision book, you can find images of the crystals mentioned to print out and stick on to the pages or glue small, flat crystals on to the front cover or inside some of the pages.

When you have added a decent number of pictures to the book, "activate" it by placing crystals of your choice on to either the front cover or each page and stating your intentions using the affirmations for each crystal listed or creating your own.

5. Pregnancy Crystal Communication Ritual

You can connect and communicate energetically with your unborn baby, and crystals can help. Once you are pregnant, take regular time to pause and reflect on the miracle occurring in your body. Give gratitude for and feel the joy in the life growing within. Hold your hands to your belly, breathe deeply, and smile. This simple act is a way to communicate with your baby on a basic level and give nourishing love energy through your hands to your womb, as your palms are connected to your heart chakra.

To communicate further, you can do a meditation similar to the fertility meditation on pages 137–139, except that a growing abdomen can make placing crystals on your belly difficult! You can hold crystals to your abdomen, or you can wear a fitted top and tuck the crystals underneath so that they are held there against your skin. Focus on the crystal of choice and feel its supportive energy being drawn inside you, nourishing you and the baby.

You could use rose quartz for love of your child, mookaite for spiritual communication and physical well-being, or pink agate for parent-and-child bonding. Say, "I love and support you and welcome you into my life." Feel free to say the baby's name if you have chosen one, or say "Baby," "Child," "Darling," or any word that feels right to you. Be open to feelings or insights that come to you. You can even ask, "Do you wish to communicate anything today?" and then listen for any answers. If none come, do not worry. Just trust that all is well. You may get a feeling that there is something you need to attend to in your diet or lifestyle or something that may benefit you, such as a type of class or therapy, so listen for helpful tips and trust your inner healer. You also can use this time to talk to your baby. Tell them what you are looking forward to, what life will be like for them, about your family, where you live, how they will enjoy their life with you as their mother. You also can do this in a letter, while keeping your crystals close by or holding one as you write.

Another way to meditate and communicate is to simply lie semi-reclined or be seated while holding a crystal of choice in one hand, rub it gently in circles over your belly, and then hold it in your palm next to you. Feel the energetic vibration of the crystal, notice what sensations it brings, and tune in to the energy. It is not uncommon for crystals to throb, pulse, or vibrate against your skin. See this as your baby's energetic heartbeat being transmitted through the crystal to you and communicating with you more deeply. Enjoy the beautiful connection.

After doing these techniques, you may wish to jot down any ideas, insights, or feelings that came to you and act on anything you feel is beneficial.

6. **Crystal Photo Frame**

Make a crystal photo frame for your future baby. Get yourself a plain frame with flat edges, and glue on a selection of crystals around the border. Add any picture that feels good when you look at it as a way to joyfully anticipate conceiving or your baby's arrival. It could be a photo of you and your partner; a cut-out image of something resembling growth, nourishment, or new life; or a positive quote. When your baby is born, add their photo to the frame.

7. **Complementary Tools to Use with These Crystals**

   ☀ Essential Oils

   For fertility: frankincense, geranium, lavender, patchouli, rosemary, ylang-ylang, cedarwood

   For pregnancy: Some essential oils should not be used in pregnancy, so always research and check before doing so, and dilute and take a "less is more" approach. Practice extra caution in the first trimester, and use oils only in spritzers or diffusers rather than applied to the skin.

   Citrus oils such as lime can be good for morning sickness, as can mandarin and lavender. Chamomile, orange, and lemon can be used throughout pregnancy.

   For labor: frankincense and clary sage

☀ Herbs, Diet, and Natural Medicine

When preparing to conceive, use natural cleaning and cosmetic products, avoid additive-laden processed foods, and stick to a diet of naturally sourced, nourishing foods with adequate protein, healthy fats, and plenty of vegetables. Seeing a qualified naturopathic practitioner for support with diet, herbs, and supplements can be helpful in cases of fertility difficulties, especially those relating to hormone imbalances and irregular ovulation. Talk to your doctor to make sure any health issues are being managed in the best way for your situation when trying to conceive.

☀ Energy Healing

Sometimes an energy healing session with an experienced and intuitive therapist can assist fertility by clearing negative thought patterns affecting the body or blockages in your energy flow to your reproductive organs due to various reasons, including fear and disappointment. Restoring and enhancing energy flow through your chakras and body may be an effective adjunct to your diet, lifestyle, and crystal regime.

☀ Journaling

Preparing for pregnancy and becoming a parent come with many emotions and thoughts that need to be processed and expressed, and writing them down can help you cope with any difficulties along the journey or simply allow you to release any fears and give gratitude for the opportunity. Consider making a fertility or pregnancy diary to record your impressions, and to allow yourself to receive answers and insights that can help you raise your vibration and create an optimal energetic environment for your baby to thrive.

8. Use the affirmations listed for each crystal, whether you have the crystal or not.

10 FINANCIAL ABUNDANCE

The Value of Financial Abundance

Financial abundance is something that many people strive for, because it can bring more freedom to your life. There is nothing wrong with wanting to pursue this, and it does not have to be associated with greed or power. It is a way to provide for your family and yourself, live comfortably, give to others and make a difference, and enjoy the freedom of spontaneity and travel.

When it comes to attracting financial abundance, focus on what it means to you and what value it brings to your life and others, rather than on the actual position of having money in your bank account.

What Does Financial Abundance Mean to Me?

You might agree with the above on what financial abundance means to you, or you might have a simpler or even more detailed answer. Always look beyond the numbers to the meaning and purpose behind it. Do you simply like having enough to pay all your bills with a bit left over for fun or having plenty of money in your account as a backup for emergencies? In either case, abundance means security for you. Or perhaps you like having a regular cash flow for doing anything you like whenever you like, in which case it means freedom. You also may like having funds

available to invest in ongoing education and courses to improve
your knowledge, skills, or personal development, in which case
money means growth and wisdom to you. Or maybe your main
purpose with money is to share it with loved ones or those in
need around the world, making generosity your meaning.

Ask yourself the following questions to find out more about
what financial abundance means to you so that when you are
working with this topic, you have a better grasp of what it
actually is you are trying to achieve or attract.

> Am I satisfied with the amount of money I
> currently have and/or that is coming into my life
> at the moment? Answer one of the following:
>
> *Yes, completely.*
>
> *Mostly, but could do with more.*
>
> *Not much.*
>
> *Not at all. I am desperate.*
>
> (If you are not completely satisfied, I
> recommend doing the abundance diary
> activity detailed on page 154, to help with
> getting into an abundance mind-set.)
>
> What is the minimum amount of money that
> would make a beneficial difference to me for
> the week ahead?
>
> What is the minimum amount of money that
> would make a beneficial difference to me for
> the next year?

Why do I feel I need more money?

If I received a one thousand dollar gift, what would I do with it?

If I received a ten thousand dollar gift, what would I do with it?

If I received a one million dollar gift, what would I do with it?

If I received one million dollars every year for the next five years, what would I do with it?

Based on your answers to the above questions, what are your money priorities and what meaning do these have for you? For example, security, generosity, freedom, life experience, knowledge, creating, legacy, fun and enjoyment, etc.

Write this into a statement: "For me, financial abundance equals . . . (freedom to be me and enjoy my life, making a difference in the world and leaving a legacy, being secure and stable in my life, etc.)."

How Can Crystals Support My Abundance?

Crystals have a great deal of natural high-vibration energy, which makes them natural abundance attractors, and some are more specific to this purpose. Certain crystals, with their particular pattern of resonance, can align you with the essence of abundance and tune out negative perceptions around money. Some can help you associate abundance with feelings of joy and happiness rather than worry or insecurity. By connecting you

with natural vibrations and feelings of abundance, they can assist you in attracting more abundance.

Which Crystals Are Good for Attracting Financial Abundance?

Any crystal that helps you feel good and raises your vibration will assist with abundance in all forms. Specifically for financial abundance, certain crystals have a particular importance. You can use crystals that relate not only to abundance itself but also to the *purpose* or *meaning* that is important for you when it comes to money, such as generosity and love or creating more opportunities for wisdom or feeling secure. In addition, if you have blocks or negative thoughts about money, you can work on this particular issue using crystals known for releasing negative patterns of thought or negative influences from your environment.

Four crystals that have a particular affinity for financial abundance include citrine (the stronger the yellow color, the better), aventurine, pyrite, and jade.

CITRINE

This crystal comes in varying depths of yellow (with bits of white), from light and bright to a deep, earthy, yellow-mustard color. The stronger the color, the better, when it comes to its powerful properties. Citrine is a "happy" stone, bringing sunshine and abundance into your life. It is a natural attractor of financial gifts, rewards, and abundance opportunities, and when paired with your intentions, it can be a powerful part of your manifesting strategies. It is particularly helpful for bringing good thoughts, instead of worry, about money, so use this stone when finances are causing you stress. Other benefits include its cleansing effects on your body and the environment and as a stimulator of creativity and joy. It can help bring useful information and insights to life through communication and expression, allowing the transference of wisdom.

- Abundance attractor
- Happiness and joy
- Cleansing and balancing
- Energizing

✿ **Affirmation for Citrine** ✿
"Financial abundance is always
flowing happily into my life."

AVENTURINE

The light-green variation of this stone is most common. However, it also can be found in blue and earthy-red colors. Filled with positive energy, it attracts vibrations of abundance and prosperity. It helps develop a healthy relationship with money and making use of it in a love-based way. Known for bringing good luck, aventurine can facilitate positive opportunities for success. It aids in releasing negative perceptions around money, thereby clearing obstacles and making way for a rich journey ahead.

* Attracts abundance and prosperity
* Clears negative feelings around money
* Brings confidence and good luck
* Brings new, positive perceptions

☙ Affirmation for Aventurine ❧
*"Opportunities for abundance always
find their way to me."*

PYRITE

You only need to look at this opulent gold crystal (also known as "fool's gold") to know it is something special. It naturally holds and radiates abundant energy and draws it in. It encourages feelings of confidence and worthiness to allow you to achieve your goals and accomplish tasks. It is helpful to use in the workplace to enhance abundance and success, and during study for concentration and memory, while assisting in keeping out negative influences.

- Success magnet
- Energy magnifier
- Confidence and worthiness
- Productivity and concentration

↬ **Affirmation for Pyrite** ↫
*"I am aligned with the magnificent essence
of financial abundance."*

JADE

Jade is a calming and healing stone. It comes in varying colors, but it is most often recognized as a muted light-green stone with some darker variations and a soapy appearance, although some specimens have dark veins and reddish-brown patches. Jade is known for bringing good luck and opportunities and connections that can help with abundance and prosperity. It also is an integrator of mind and body. It helps with physical healing while encouraging the mind to be more positive and impacting health in that way too.

- Good-luck stone
- Abundance and prosperity
- Stress relief
- Healing and cleansing from negative energy

↬ **Affirmation for Jade** ↫
*"Each new day brings me good luck
and prosperity."*

How Can I Use These Crystals for My Financial Abundance?

Place abundance crystals in the natural environment around you, in areas where growth occurs, such as next to flowers or plants.

Put a flat slice of citrine in your purse or wallet, next to your cards and money, to act as an energetic money magnet.

Use a citrine key ring so that you welcome abundance into your home when you unlock the door and attract it while out and about.

Take aventurine to job interviews, bank or investment appointments, or meetings to enhance good luck and opportunities for abundance.

Keep pyrite and a raw citrine cluster in the left-hand (abundance) corner of your office or home.

Crystal Activities for Financial Abundance

1. **An Abundant Welcome**

    Create a welcome zone for abundance at your front door, to signal that you are ready to receive. Place a potted plant on the doorstep and put citrine crystals on top of the soil or around the stem of the plant. This combines crystal energy with earth energy and symbolizes the growth of abundance. You also can do this inside your front door, and even add a variety of crystals to the pot. A Welcome mat is a nice touch, too, to enhance the effect.

2. **Abundance Diary**
    Using a brand-new journal or notebook and a pen in either red or a color that you love to enhance the energy through the high vibration of color, create an abundance diary. Every day, for at least thirty days to start with, write down at least three things that represent abundance for you and that you are grateful for or appreciate. They can be directly related to money or be symbolic. The more you notice the abundance in your life, the more you bring into your life.

    Examples for your diary could be: *I found money on the sidewalk, someone treated me to a coffee, the flowers I planted began to bloom, I got a bonus at work, I enjoyed an abundance of laughter, a friend got a new high-paying job.* (Being grateful for others' abundance helps too.)

    To use the power of crystals, place your diary when not in use in the left-hand corner of your house or room, with one or more crystals on top of it. And when recording your abundance list each day, hold a citrine crystal in one hand while writing with the other or simply have it next to you or resting on the opposite page like a paperweight. As the first thirty days pass, watch what happens and enjoy the increasing abundance in your life!

3. **Number Eight**
    Utilize the number eight whenever and wherever possible, because this number relates to abundance, especially when in triple form: 888. Eight is the infinity symbol, representing endless abundance and the continual flow of the energy of

life. You can display abundance crystals in groups of eight
or use a crystal grid with eight sections. You also can create
an infinity or number eight symbol by arranging crystals
into that shape. In addition, say your abundance-related
affirmations or intentions eight times.

4. Crystal Grid Abundance Ceremony

Create a grid or number eight/infinity pattern with the crystals
mentioned in this chapter and with any others relating to
abundance. You can print out a sacred geometry pattern or
use a cloth or wooden grid, a round plate or tray, or anything
flat to arrange your crystals. You could use a piece of pyrite
or a quartz or citrine generator (pointed tip) in the center. Use
jade and/or aventurine in the outer parts to draw in luck and
prosperity and radiate it outward, and the citrine to connect
the outer crystals with the centerpiece. You might like to add
small flowers and even seeds to your grid, or sprinkle tiny
crystal chips of citrine, quartz, or rose quartz to amplify the
positive energy and symbolize abundance through the higher
number of crystals.

When complete, light a candle and take some deep
breaths. Declare an intention of gratitude about abundance,
such as "Thank you for the increasing financial abundance
in my life." Then state what abundance means to you and
what you are looking forward to receiving. For example:
"I now welcome an abundant regular income into my life,
bringing stability, security, and freedom to be enjoyed by
myself and others."

You may keep your grid on display, if you wish, in the far left-hand corner of your house or room, or on a crystal altar, or on a table in your office. You do not need to keep it displayed for it to work because you have already gathered, focused, and radiated the energy of your intention through the crystals. But keeping it active for at least twenty-four hours is helpful to allow some momentum.

5. **Complementary Tools and Tips to Use with Crystals**
   Hold on to winning scratch-off lottery tickets a little while longer before redeeming them, because they are great examples that surprise abundance can occur and can help attract more of the same.

   Always *keep a coin or bill in your pocket or purse* to have the energy of abundance with you at all times. It is even better when paired with a small citrine stone.

   Keep your plants watered and nourished, and regularly display a vase of fresh flowers in your home.

6. **Use the affirmations listed for each crystal whenever you need an abundance boost, whether you have the crystal or not.**

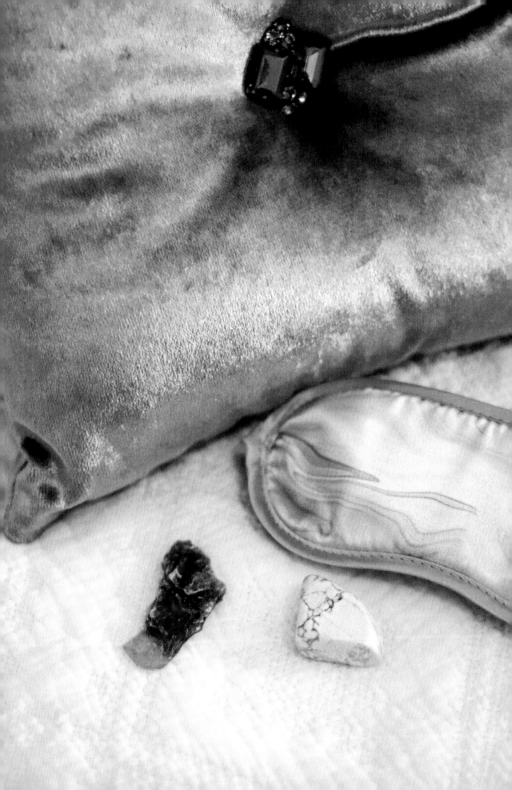

11 SLEEP AND DREAMS

Why Good Sleep Is Essential

It is clear to all of us that sleep is not just downtime or rest for the body, but that it is an essential part of our life that helps us rejuvenate, repair, heal, and maintain our body, mind, and spirit. Sleep is so important that we cannot survive without it, and prolonged sleep deprivation has damaging consequences. Sleep is not just about quantity but also quality. Most people function best on about seven-and-a-half hours of sleep, or the equivalent of five sleep cycles (ninety minutes per cycle), which is why we tend to round it off to a good eight hours to allow extra dozing time. Many people often feel they need more, usually because of poor sleep quality or of sleep debt, whereby a person has accumulated a lack of sleep over time and needs to gradually make it up each night by adding more cycles to their total sleep time.

During sleep, certain hormones and metabolic activities increase while others decrease, and our immune system kicks into high gear to repair any cell damage and fight off any roaming microbes. Our body and nervous system get to slow down and rest, while our spiritual self heightens and our connection to our source is stronger because the mind does not interfere.

Overall, good sleep is one of life's greatest gifts, helping us in our waking hours with just about everything!

The Purpose of Dreams

One of the wonders of being human is the awareness of having dreams, though recall of most dreams often disappears soon after waking. Dreams can be pleasant, amusing, surprising, weird, or scary. When we experience them, they feel real, and it is not uncommon to feel genuine emotions on waking. Even if we are not physically in the dream experience, we are there emotionally and spiritually, so the brain perceives it as real.

Dreams are said to be nature's way of processing all the things we experience in daily life, to filter our experiences and sort through them, discarding some sensory memories and storing others while linking them all together and adding to our memory database. Dreams are said to be our direct connection to the spiritual world, where our receptivity opens up more and we can receive messages and insights or even visits from those who have passed over.

Dreams appear to be necessary for good health and are a fascinating subject in their own right, with dream interpretation being a popular area of study.

How Can Crystals Improve My Sleep?

Certain crystals can help improve your sleep by radiating vibrational frequencies that support relaxation. They may assist by reducing fear and anxiety and excessive thoughts, allowing your mind to "switch off" more easily and/or maintain a state conducive to sleep throughout the night. They also can simply be a way to remind yourself that it is sleep time, by serving as a prompt or cue to train the mind to relax and prepare for rest. For example, pick up a crystal beside your bed and hold it for a moment to "tell" your body it is time for sleep, just like winding down with a book or having a relaxing bath does.

Which Crystals Are Good for Improving Sleep and Recalling Dreams?

Not all crystals can help with our sleep and dreams. Some disturb sleep due to their exuberant energy, so it is important to be aware of their properties and to allow for trial and error to see what works for you.

Four crystals that can help improve sleep and/or dream recall are white howlite, lepidolite, amethyst, and Herkimer diamond.

WHITE HOWLITE

With a pure white appearance and light-gray veins, white howlite is calming just to look at and a great bedside companion. It can remind you to simplify your life and get back to your main priorities and self-care, by reducing anxiety and tension and aiding in relaxation and sleep. Symbolizing purity, peace, and calm, white howlite is the stone to help you release worries and excess thoughts, bringing you back to a sense of balance. It will help you stay attuned to your true nature and to serenity and assist with preparing you for restful sleep.

- Reducing anxiety and worry
- Relaxation and calm
- Reducing insomnia and aiding restful sleep
- Purity and peaceful awareness

Power Point… Howlite also comes in a blue color, and because white howlite is a good absorber of dye, it is sometimes artificially colored and falsely sold as turquoise. So be aware of a stone's authenticity.

꙳ Affirmation for White Howlite ꙳
"I am calm and peaceful, ready for soothing sleep."

LEPIDOLITE

Lepidolite is the crystal of serenity and has a unique and subtle beauty with its soft pinky-lilac hues. It is used as either a tumbled stone or in slices or shards with a glassy appearance and fragility. Mineral rich in constitution, it contains lithium, one of the ingredients in mood-stabilizing medicines. Lepidolite helps when you feel stuck or trapped by your emotions and negative patterns, allowing your difficulties to be seen with new eyes and a healthier perspective. It will assist with clear thinking, taking away excessive thoughts and overwhelming feelings and calming down your nervous system, especially before sleep. It is great for work-related stress in a high-technology environment, which may be contributing to insomnia, because it helps to balance out the effects of electromagnetic frequencies with stabilizing and calming ones.

- Calming and serenity
- Stabilizing and settling before sleep
- Clear thinking and planning
- Balancing effect in a high-technology environment

To help you fully embrace the power of lepidolite for serenity and sleep, read this message as though it is coming from a treasured friend.

Dear Friend,

You need not take on all the worries of the world. You are allowed to surrender and let the universe work it all out. I will help you remember the peace within you, the calm and serene sense of being that carries you through emotional difficulties. Tune in to that serenity at any time, knowing it is there and that all is well. With serenity comes clarity, and with clarity comes knowing and purpose, helping you to move forward and make progress with ease. My presence at bedtime can help you prepare for restorative sleep, so you can wake with a calm enthusiasm for the day ahead.

Remember, just breathe. Then breathe again and know that everything will be okay.

Love,

Lepidolite

≈ Affirmation for Lepidolite ≈
"Serenity washes through my mind and body,
and I am safe and secure while I sleep."

AMETHYST

One of the most popular and well-known crystals is amethyst, which is recognized by its natural purple color. Amethyst is widely available. It is often worn as jewelry and used with the body as tumbled stones and points or as clusters and geodes for displaying. Some geodes are huge and give off an amazing energy. This is the crystal of intuition, calm and balance, clarity, and linking the physical to the spiritual. It is helpful in cases of illness, assisting with overall balancing of the body systems and emotional state. It calms overthinking, connects you with your source, and helps with overnight healing processes, so it is particularly useful for health conditions that are impacting on sleep. It can be very effective in enhancing meditation, particularly as part of a presleep ritual.

- Intuition and insight
- Calming and restful
- Overall balancing effect
- Transmits positive high vibrations to surroundings

⁂ Affirmation for Amethyst ∾
*"I am supported by source as I sleep
and nourished by a calm and constant
connection to spirit."*

HERKIMER DIAMOND

This is a type of quartz crystal with two pointy ends (double terminated) and natural facets, giving it the appearance of a diamond. It is named after the region it is found in: Herkimer, New York. It is usually clear in color, but it also can come in a smoky yellow variation and is great for treating insomnia and recalling dreams. It is especially good when sleep issues or nightmares are due to environmental stress or electromagnetic radiation because it protects from and normalizes these imbalanced frequencies. With dream recall, it helps connect to higher spiritual energies and collective consciousness so that dreams are vivid and can be understood. In the process, it enhances psychic abilities as well as remote connection between people, making it useful during readings or distant healings. It can be a good stone to use in the bedroom to aid healthy sleep and insightful dreams.

- Sleep enhancer
- Recalling dreams
- Understanding and awareness
- Spiritual and psychic connection

> ❧ Affirmation for Herkimer Diamond ❦
> *"My dreams are clear and insightful,
> helping me in both my sleep
> and waking hours."*

How Can I Use These Crystals for My Sleep?

Place them directly under your pillow at night, trying out one crystal at a time to see how each affects you.

Do a presleep or dream recall meditation, holding your chosen crystals or placing one on your third eye (forehead).

Have jewelry that you wear only at bedtime, and put it on a couple of hours beforehand to help you wind down.

Turn on a Himalayan salt lamp in the hours prior to sleep, with crystals placed beside it.

Crystal Activities for Sleep and Dreams

1. Create a Sleep Kit

Have a small bowl or container or a fabric sachet or bag to hold your sleep crystals next to your bed. You also can keep them under your pillow. First, cleanse them in the sun and/or under the full moon before using them, to clear any built-up energy they may have absorbed. You can have other items conducive to sleep next to your bed, such as a sleep mask to block out light, a soft lamp or candle, earplugs, a book of positive quotes or affirmations, and essential oils or aromatherapy cream containing lavender.

2. Presleep Ritual

Create a presleep ritual that makes you feel calm and peaceful. When you do a ritual like this regularly, your brain will start to expect it and your body will respond accordingly, allowing you to relax more easily and quickly and your sleep to improve over time. Crystals are great for rituals because they help focus your thoughts and intentions into the physical world and strengthen your energetic connection with the spiritual world.

Decide what is important for your sleep ritual and then choose your crystals accordingly or simply use the recommended ones in this chapter. For example, if

you often feel overwhelmed with excessive thoughts
and worries before bedtime or feel like you have not
accomplished enough during the day, lepidolite might work
well for you to help with serenity and peace. Or if you
have insomnia and toss and turn a lot, try white howlite.
If you mainly want to boost your sleep efficiency, overall
health, and energy during the day, try amethyst. If health
issues are disrupting your sleep, see the health and healing
section on pages 31–40 for more specific options to deal
with the underlying aspects of your concerns.

Your ritual can consist of one or more of the
following, in the order or sequence that feels right to you,
and done in addition to any other presleep tasks, such as
bathing or showering, reading, or spending time with your
partner.

❀ Crystal Affirmations

Hold your chosen crystals, state your affirmations
or intentions (out loud, preferably), feel them to be
true. You may wish to place the crystal to your heart,
your third eye (forehead), or in your hand. Use the
affirmation listed for the specific crystal or create
your own.

❀ Journaling

With a simple notebook or journal specifically for your
sleep ritual, write down any thoughts or worries you
wish to release from your mind and then rip the paper
out and throw it away, handing over your concerns to

the universe. You also may like to jot down a gratitude list or things you are looking forward to and leave this page in the journal. You can record your crystal affirmations, as well.

Lighting and Atmosphere

Your sleep environment is important, so make sure you maximize yours to assist with good rest. Dim the lights or use a red night-light or salt lamp or a few candles, if you wish to read or journal. (Be sure to blow out the candles before you get too sleepy!) You also can utilize a regular soft lamp and wear blue light–blocking glasses, because blue light can interfere with your normal sleep hormones. Make sure the temperature of the room is comfortable—not too hot or too cold—but more on the cooler side. Enhance the atmosphere with relaxing music and essential oils, and make sure any technology is switched off or put away.

Meditation/Visualization

Before you sleep, you may do a short seated meditation and then lie down, or you may meditate lying down. If seated, hold the crystals in your hands. If reclined, place one of your crystals on your third eye (forehead) and the other over your heart. You can put soft and smooth crystals inside a pair of socks during the night. Just be careful when getting out of bed and remember to remove them so they don't hurt your feet or cause instability when you walk.

Breathe slowly and visualize yourself waking up refreshed and ready for the day. See yourself doing well throughout the following day and getting into bed that night feeling well and happy. You can use this time to visualize any specific goals, dreams, or intentions because the times before sleep and waking from sleep are very powerful for manifesting.

It can help to write down your ritual steps for easy reference and as a reminder until it becomes second nature. A presleep ritual can help you relax more easily and sleep in unfamiliar surroundings when you travel.

3. **Dream Recall and Journaling**
Using a piece of Herkimer diamond or amethyst, set an intention before going to sleep that you will remember a dream and ask spirit to help you. Spirit, source energy, or universal consciousness is always available to tune in to when needed, and genuine requests for assistance are always heard. Place the crystal under your pillow or beside your bed, on top of a piece of paper or a notebook, along with a pen, and when you wake, jot down anything that comes to you. Try not to analyze or describe in too much detail. Focus first on key words that represent images, feelings, or things that happened before your conscious mind kicks in and your subconscious takes away the memories. The more you note your dreams, the easier it gets to recall them and to be aware of any recurrences or

messages that may come through for your benefit. When you do remember, hold the crystal and give thanks for its assistance.

Dream journaling can be done visually, if you like, by drawing anything you saw or creating an abstract image of how your dream felt.

4. A Note on Using Sleep Crystals with Children

Be sure that they are old enough to not put crystals in their mouth. Use the crystals together before sleep as a relaxing ritual, and then take them out of the room with you.

12 CHAKRA BALANCING AND ENERGY HEALING

What Are Chakras and Why Is Balance Important?

Chakras are the energy centers in our body that are focused into specific areas. They are all connected to one another and to the energy around us. Chakras are like a channel system, and they are a way for the dynamic energy, which is not seen but that supports life from the spiritual realm, to flow through the body.

Each chakra is associated with a particular area of the body and a specific emotion. They can become blocked or imbalanced, disrupting the optimal flow of healing energy and contributing to various issues within the associated areas. Energy healers can tune in to these imbalances and help restore flow and balance, as can your own inner healing abilities, especially with the help of crystals.

What Is Energy Healing?

Energy healing is a way of working with the energy that is part of all things. It is about helping to adjust the flow of energy to certain areas of the body and modifying the vibration to one that matches a healthier frequency, so the body is assisted at a deeper level than just the physical.

Emotions have vibrations, too, so it can involve healing emotional imbalances that may be affecting overall health and well-being. This is done by focusing high-vibration healing energy

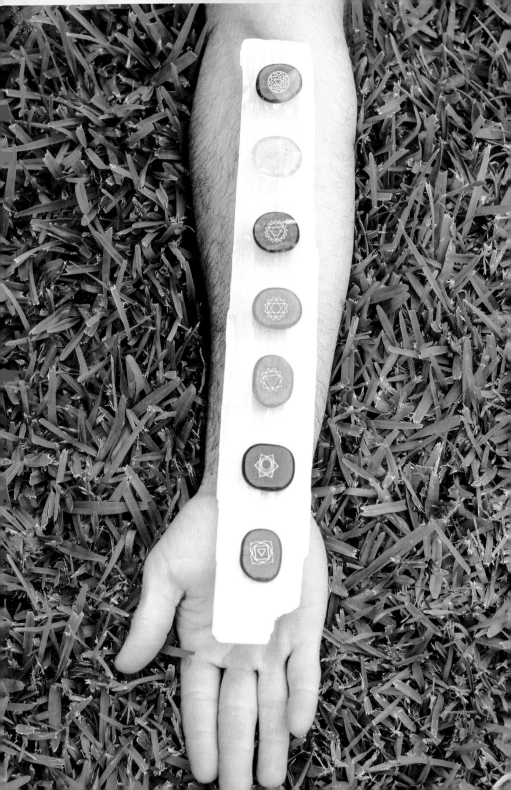

(through the hands, intentions, and/or crystals) to particular areas of the body, so they receive a healthy supply of energetic nourishment. Overall, energy healing can help clear negative energy, improve flow of stagnant energy, and input more positive source energy.

How Can Crystals Help Balance My Chakras and Energy System?

Because crystals have high vibrational frequencies, they can have a positive impact on the energy flow in your chakras. Different chakras correspond to different colors, and crystals can be used for specific chakras based on their color and properties. Using crystals in energy healing and chakra balancing can encourage the frequency within the chakras to match and embed their beneficial properties within the energy system.

The Seven Main Chakras

Crown Chakra: located at the top of the head; associated with spiritual connection

Third Eye Chakra: located between the eyebrows; associated with intuition and insight and being able to see the complete picture

Throat Chakra: located in the throat/neck area; associated with communication and expressing your truth

Heart Chakra: located in the chest area; associated with love and acceptance of self and others

Solar Plexus Chakra: located in the lower part of the rib cage; associated with self-confidence and self-worth

Sacral Chakra: located just below the navel; associated with sexuality and pleasure and being open to new experiences and opportunities

Base/Root Chakra: located in the lower part of the spine or on top of the pubic bone area of the pelvis; associated with groundedness, stability, and financial security

Which Crystals Are Good for Chakra Balancing and Energy Healing?

There are many crystals that can help balance the chakras, depending on which need the most attention. Once you know the colors that represent each chakra, it is easy to select crystals because it is often a matter of choosing one with the same or similar color. However, you can use a crystal of a different color if the properties relate to that chakra. For example, the heart chakra is green, but you can use pink rose quartz as well as green crystals.

Colors and Crystals That Relate to Each Chakra

Crown Chakra: violet; amethyst, quartz, ametrine, serpentine, apophyllite, diamond

Third Eye Chakra: indigo; sodalite, amethyst, lapis lazuli

Throat Chakra: blue; blue lace agate, blue calcite, turquoise, lapis lazuli

Heart Chakra: green; aventurine, jade, peridot, rose quartz

Solar Plexus Chakra: yellow; citrine, yellow jasper, amber

Sacral Chakra: orange; tiger's eye, carnelian, amber

Base/Root Chakra: red; red jasper, garnet, ruby, hematite

Seven common chakra crystals are ametrine, lapis lazuli, blue calcite, peridot, yellow jasper, amber, and red jasper.

AMETRINE

This crystal is a combination of amethyst and citrine, giving it the properties of both, as well as its own unique benefits. It taps you into universal abundance, especially when used with the crown chakra, helping you gain awareness and insight into any blocks that prevent you from achieving your potential. It also can be used with the solar plexus. Ametrine allows you to see beyond the physical, assisting with greater understanding of situations and knowing how to approach them best. It calms the mind and enhances positive emotions and increases your spiritual and psychic mindfulness when used during meditation, while bringing a greater awareness into your everyday life and interactions with others.

- Crown and sacral chakras
- Connects to universal abundance
- Awareness and positive perception
- Focus and calmness
- Spiritual awakening

ॐ **Affirmation for Ametrine** ॐ
"I am tuned into my universal support system."

LAPIS LAZULI

This rich royal-blue crystal with gold-colored flecks is an amazingly powerful stone for mental and spiritual wisdom, bringing clarity to any situation and the ability to express yourself truthfully and authentically. It helps you to tune in to universal intelligence, the greatest teacher, and boost your intuition and psychic abilities, while providing strength and connectedness to your environment so that you may integrate wisdom and truth into your life.

Lapis lazuli balances the throat chakra, which allows for assured communication and self-expression, speaking the truth without fear. It lets you use your intuition to guide you through life's learning experiences as well as stimulates effective communication. It also nurtures listening so that communication may be two-way and more balanced.

* Third eye and throat chakra
* Wisdom and insight
* Inner power and confidence
* Communication and expression
* Intuition and guidance

☙ Affirmation for Lapis Lazuli ☙
"I enjoy confident, capable, and intuitive self-expression."

BLUE CALCITE

This pale-blue crystal is soapy to the touch and like a soothing elixir to the body, mind, and soul. It helps to balance the throat chakra and supports calm communication. It allows you to rest and recover from intense periods of expression and release and to regain your soul's voice, preventing a tendency to overdo or overexplain things. It assists with calming the nerves during public speaking and keeps communication flowing freely and smoothly. Blue calcite is cleansing for mind and body, through its subtle but powerful filtering properties, allowing it to give off positive and healing energy. It is beneficial to use after chaotic experiences to calm and recenter the self and allow for rest and stillness, so the spiritual realm can restore the physical.

- Throat chakra
- Soothing and healing
- Clear communication
- Restorative
- Cleansing

❧ Affirmation for Blue Calcite ☙
"I am soothed by the nourishing flow of spirit."

PERIDOT

This is a yellowish-green crystal that resonates with and soothes the heart chakra and helps the solar plexus when issues of the heart have affected self-esteem. It is powerful for removing old energy, cleansing, and clearing to make way for new and positive energy. It is strong in its ability to let go of the past, giving off a clear and light vibration that has no room for heavy energies. It teaches the wisdom of the heart and living from a place of authentic truth, shining your light on others to illuminate their own heart. When it is time to move forward without delay, this is the crystal to help you do that.

- Positive and rapid transformation
- Emotional healer
- Cleansing and revitalizing
- Strength and authentic identity

⊱ Affirmation for Peridot ⊰
"I am open to rapid and positive transformation."

YELLOW JASPER

Jaspers are grounding stones that stabilize and center the self into the foundation of Mother Earth. Yellow jasper encourages the enjoyment of life and keeps the mind positive about its process and outcomes, knowing that all will be well. It helps you to feel supported in life and nurtured, from the outside and within, as it increases your feelings of self-worth and self-esteem. Yellow jasper also can settle the stomach when nervous situations arise. Jasper guides logical thinking and problem-solving, helping you to organize your thoughts and ideas and giving you the persistence to see things through.

- Solar plexus chakra
- Grounding and stability
- Positive mind-set
- Persistence and perseverance
- Settles nerves

⊱ Affirmation for Yellow Jasper ⊰
"I am nurtured at all times."

AMBER

A warm golden-yellowy brown color, amber is a solidified resin from trees and contains soothing energy from the earth, bringing negativity and waste to the surface to be removed and flushing away toxins and inflammation. It encourages self-healing of the body, transmitting the right frequency for ideal functioning and regeneration and for dealing with pain. It is helpful for when physical issues are caused by or made worse by a negative or low state of mind, lifting and brightening the mind-set so that the body can respond accordingly. Amber is a grounding stone, alleviating feelings of being overwhelmed and disconnection by restoring awareness and links to earth energy and strength.

- Solar plexus and sacral chakras
- Physical cleanser and detoxifier
- Encourages the body's healing systems
- Uplifts the mood
- Grounds the body and mind

▸ Affirmation for Amber ◂
"My body is clean, healthy, and stable."

RED JASPER

This earthy-red crystal is a solid-looking stone with properties that enhance stability and security. All jasper crystals have a grounding effect, helping you feel a strong connection to Mother Earth and nurturing the body while stabilizing the emotions. Red jasper alleviates loneliness and disconnectedness, brings feelings of safety and belonging, and encourages you to see the unity of all people and your place in the world. Emotionally, it delivers strength during times of hardship and fluctuation, letting a natural balance occur and settling overactive responses. With its stabilizing effects, it supports endurance and the ability to keep going, withstands the effects of chronic stress, and allows for a consistency of determination and strength.

- Base/root chakra
- Grounding and security
- Stabilizes the emotions
- Supports feelings of belonging and connection
- Balancing and settling effects

> ❧ Affirmation for Red Jasper ❧
> *"I am stable and grounded within myself
> and the world around me."*

How Can I Use These Crystals for My Chakras and Energy System?

Meditate with chakra crystals placed on your body or alongside you at the level where each chakra is. You can get separate crystals that are suggested for each chakra or a chakra kit with crystals that have a different symbol representing each chakra engraved on them.

Focus different intentions or affirmations on each chakra crystal, holding each one in your hand or around the associated body area.

Wear a chakra bracelet or pendant containing crystals for each of the seven chakras to help keep them balanced as you go about your day.

Create a chakra crystal grid or place seven chakra stones on a long platform such as a selenite slab or a plate or a table, and then hold your hands over each stone one at a time and breathe in the energy, imagining it being drawn up into you.

Ask your intuition to guide you as to which chakras may be needing more attention at any one time. Then do a crystal-based meditation and visualization on that area to encourage free energy flow.

Notice what colors you feel drawn to in your surroundings. It can be an indicator of which chakra needs attention and/or which crystal would benefit you most. For example, being drawn to reddish colors may point to your base or sacral chakra. Purples may point to your third eye or throat chakra. Use a crystal associated with the color calling you.

You can purchase yoga or meditation mats and towels with chakra symbols or colors on them to lie on while doing your crystal and chakra meditations.

Crystal Activities for Chakra Balance and Energy Healing

1. Seven-Day Chakra Cleanse
    Focus on one chakra per day, holding a crystal in your hand or around the chakra and saying affirmations or intentions

associated with it. Do at least one activity that supports that chakra, based on its purpose and meaning. For example, for the base chakra, do a grounding activity such as walking barefoot in nature.

Start with the base chakra on day one, and work your way up over seven days. Choose a crystal for each, and try the following affirmations and activities or create your own.

Day 1: Base "I am grounded, stable, and secure
within myself."
Activity: Walk barefoot in nature.

Day 2: Sacral "I am open to receiving and
enjoying all of life's gifts."
Activity: Do something you love, purely for the pleasure of it.

Day 3: Solar Plexus "I am capable and
confident."
Activity: Write a list of ten things you are good at and/or ten positive traits you possess.

Day 4: Heart "I embody and radiate
unconditional love."
Activity: Show love to someone by saying you love and appreciate them or by pointing out something you love about them (their smile, their kindness, their laugh, their dedication).

Day 5: Throat "I confidently and clearly express
my true self."

Activity: Compose a letter to the universe, thanking it for all your blessings and confidently asking for what you would like to receive in your life. Or write a social media post or tell someone in person something they may not know about you: something you have learned so far in life or what you are looking forward to. Put yourself out there.

Day 6: Third Eye "I listen to and trust my intuition."
Activity: Ask your intuition what message it has for you today and then act on any guidance. Is there something you need to do, something to avoid or give closure to, or an opportunity you need to take?

Day 7: Crown "I am always connected to supportive source energy."
Activity: Meditate for a few minutes with your crystal. Breathe in the feeling of connection to your spiritual source, and breathe out any resistance or blocks. Feel the supportive and strengthening flow of energy through your whole body.

You also can do this crystal affirmation chakra cleanse in one go, as a crystal meditation or healing session, one chakra at a time, focusing on drawing energy into that chakra to balance it and moving on to the next one when it feels right. Then follow it up with one week or day full of chakra balancing activities.

2. Chakra Crystal Meditation

Ask someone to help you with this, or do your best on your own. Place seven crystals on your body where each chakra is. Lie down on your back with all of them on your belly first, and then place them in each location, starting from your base chakra. You also can place them by your side or one on each side, and then meditate next to them. Play healing music or a chakra guided meditation to assist you with tuning into each of your chakras and benefiting from a deep relaxation.

Try this once a day or once a week and see how you feel. I often find doing chakra guided meditations more restful and rejuvenating than a regular guided meditation. I think this is because it is not only allowing your mind and body to calm down, but it also is focusing on these energy centers and balancing the whole system step by step, making it a more thorough and healing session.

3. Chakra Art

Get yourself paints and a canvas or watercolors or colored pencils and paper, and make an intuitive chakra artwork. First, select a color and a crystal for each chakra. You might like to use chakra music or meditations, switching colors when each chakra is focused upon. Or if you would like to take your time and go at your own pace, create in silence or with gentle relaxation music. Start with the base chakra and a red or dark earthy color and a crystal, placing it in front of you near the canvas or paper. Paint or draw anything in whatever way you please. You might like to use rhythmic strokes, tuning in to the energy of the chakra, or add dots and blobs. See what feels natural to you and the particular chakra.

When you are ready, switch to the next chakra, swapping the crystal and color for another. Continue painting or drawing, one color and crystal at a time, until you have completed all seven chakras. Do not judge what you are creating; let it be what it will be. The main thing is to enjoy the process and lower any energetic resistance in your chakras and energy field. When finished, add any extra aspects or touch up colors that need more attention, and then have a deeper look at your artwork. How does it feel to you? Is there any message or awareness that it brings?

Display your artwork and try doing another one a month later to see how your perception and awareness of your chakras has progressed. This can be a fun activity to do with friends. Have a chakra art session, and then each person can discuss any insights that came up during the process.

13 CHILDREN AND CRYSTALS

The Power of Youth

Children have a purity of energy that is very similar to crystals, and they often connect easily and deeply to them. It is great to educate them from a young age about nature's miracles, such as crystals, which helps them learn about the earth, how things are formed, and what all living things are made of. Just like crystals, children are great absorbers of energy and information, and getting them used to having crystals around is helpful for them as they grow, keeping their vibration high and attracting positive experiences.

How Can Crystals Help Children?

Children are very receptive to energy, even if they do not realize it. Because of this, they can benefit hugely from positive crystal energy in a variety of ways, such as with learning, focus, calming, sleep, communication, protection, behavior, and health.

Children often learn well through visual and tactile stimuli, and crystals, by their nature, naturally stand out in both ways. Children find these beautiful gems intriguing, powerful, interesting, and magical.

Which Crystals Are Good for Children's Well-Being?

It is good to allow your children to choose crystals for themselves, as they will naturally be drawn to one that suits them and feels right. However, you also can use specific crystals with them to assist with common childhood needs such as courage and confidence, kindness, calmness, protection and security, and individuality. Kyanite, tiger's eye, onyx, dalmatian jasper, aquamarine, and peacock ore are good choices.

KYANITE

Kyanite is a pale, silvery-blue-and-white crystal with a shardlike stripey appearance. It repels negative energy and does not usually need cleansing, unlike other crystals, so it is a powerful one to use for maintaining a high vibration and connection to spiritual power. It embodies inner strength, courage, and truth, and helps with speaking, communication, listening, and understanding. It is perfect for children who are very sensitive or have a strong intuition, because it will guide and protect them and help them to discern between their inner voice and other people's thoughts and beliefs.

- ☀ Speaking truthfully
- ☀ Courage and inner power
- ☀ Understanding and awareness on a higher level
- ☀ Intuition

> ࣾ **Affirmation for Kyanite** ࣿ
> *"I trust myself."*

TIGER'S EYE

This crystal has browny-orange, tigerlike stripes and banding and holds a powerful energy of the earth to help ground and stabilize, while lifting the spirit to new heights and levels of awareness. It protects against conflicts and accusations, keeping the user in a state of calm and stable energy. It also helps with dedication to a task and getting things done, which can be beneficial for children who struggle with schoolwork or concentration. It is a practical stone, working to achieve physical results via spiritual support and giving confidence and courage to work through any task.

- ☀ Balancing and grounding
- ☀ Uplifting and raising awareness
- ☀ Dedication and consistency
- ☀ Protective and supportive

> ࣾ **Affirmation for Tiger's Eye** ࣿ
> *"I am courageous and positive."*

ONYX

Onyx is a black stone, sometimes with a few small white or gray patches or bands. It is not as glassy in appearance compared to obsidian, which can help to distinguish the two. Onyx makes you feel strong and stable wherever you go, protecting you from sudden changes or negative influences in your surroundings, and can therefore be helpful for difficult or stressful situations, such as starting school or dealing with social challenges or learning issues. It is also beneficial for those who are sensitive and need to feel comfortable and safe in themselves. It assists with endurance and getting through challenges and long days, while creating a balance of energies around you.

- Protection and security
- Strength and endurance
- Stress relief
- Balancing and stabilizing

Affirmation for Onyx
"I am strong and protected."

DALMATIAN JASPER

A unique-looking jasper with a light-beige base color and black spots, dalmatian jasper is a crystal that is both protective and grounding and embodies self-esteem and self-worth, helping you to be confident within yourself. It brings a joyful playfulness to life and lets you see the light and the positive in challenging situations. It is a wonderful crystal for supporting individual needs and courage to be yourself, allowing your true nature and personality to shine through without worrying what people think.

* Grounding and protection
* Joyfulness
* Puts your true self in the spotlight
* Self-confidence

Power Point . . . The black spots in dalmatian jasper are black tourmaline, one of the most protective crystals available.

> ॐ Affirmation for Dalmatian Jasper ॐ
> *"I love being me."*

AQUAMARINE

This beautiful blue crystal with a green tinge has a smooth and clear appearance and nourishes the mind with calmness and clarity. It soothes and protects, reduces negativity, and helps you to see the light in the darkness. Aquamarine provides unclouded insight into life and allows you to communicate it to others, while bringing understanding and acceptance to all interactions. It benefits those who are highly sensitive, enhancing adaptation to surroundings and resilience of heart and mind, while protecting from excess stimulation and stress. Through its calming effect and encouragement of pure thought, it delivers confidence and courage and reduces feelings of regret and being overwhelmed. Aquamarine helps you to move through daily life with ease, maintaining a strong inner foundation that negativity cannot penetrate.

- Confidence and courage
- Helps with speaking the truth
- Soothing and protective
- Releases judgment and blame

ঌ Affirmation for Aquamarine ঌ
"I am calm and peaceful."

PEACOCK ORE

Peacock ore is a unique and popular crystal with sparkly flecks of pink, blue, purple, green, and gold. It is also known as "bornite" or "chalcopyrite," and its oxidation produces the iridescence and sparkling colors. It is popular among children because of its bright, multicolored sparkles, and it stimulates feelings of happiness and joy, reminding us that anything is possible. It fosters acceptance of all differences, releases judgments, and opens up awareness and insight to allow creativity to flourish.

- Happiness and joy
- Unlimited possibilities
- Acceptance
- Awareness and insightful creativity

ঌ Affirmation for Peacock Ore ঌ
"I am unique and special."

How Can I Use These Crystals for My Child?

You can buy crystals in small animal shapes, such as frogs, elephants, cats, and dragons. These are a great way to introduce children to crystals, because they are seen as toys as well as natural specimens. You can give each animal (based on the crystal it is made from) a "superpower" to help children know how it can have a positive impact. For example, a jade frog has the superpower of healing, an agate elephant has the superpower of strength, and a tiger's eye dragon has the superpower of courage.

For children old enough to know that crystals are not candy or something to be put in the mouth, **tumbled stones are great** because they have smooth, rounded edges and feel nice to hold. Take your child to a store and let them choose one or two crystals that they feel drawn to or have them select a handful and help them narrow it down. Tell them that crystals come from nature and are very special and can make them live their best self through being positive, kind, and caring.

Many children love setting up their small toys on a shelf. You can **add crystals to a display**, as well, such as crystal towers or points to act as a kind of castle (only use sharp-pointed crystals for older children) or round flat crystals to be stepping stones for toy animals. They can even allocate a crystal for each toy.

Reading and learning can be improved with crystals; you can use one as a pointer to guide their sight along written words on a page. Get them to choose one they can call their "reading crystal."

Give your child a crystal key chain for their schoolbag or pencil case, or let them know they can keep a small crystal in their pocket to help them feel brave and confident.

Place tiger's eye, white howlite, or amethyst next to their bed to help with relaxation and sleep.

Crystal Activities for Children and Parents/Teachers

1. Schoolbag Kit

Create a special crystal kit to keep in your child's schoolbag to assist them with friendships and social interactions, feeling grounded in large crowds, focusing during class, and being comfortable and confident in their own skin. Teach them that just as each crystal is unique and has its own special gifts and appearance and positive attributes, so do they and all other children. Tell them that the crystal kit is a reminder they are wonderful just the way they are and so, too, is everyone else! Crystals can be visual reminders of the uniqueness of all individuals, while exerting their positive influence on their vibrational state.

Include any of the following as small tumbled stones in a sachet or drawstring bag:

tiger's eye for courage (to speak up, stand up for themselves, raise their hand in class, or introduce themselves to a new friend);

onyx for protection from negative influences;

dalmatian jasper to release insecurities and be brave to be themselves;

kyanite for clear thought and confidence in trusting their gut instinct; and

aquamarine for dealing with challenging people or situations with calmness and courage.

2. Treasure Hunt

As suggested in chapter 6, "Family Harmony," a crystal treasure hunt is a fun way for kids to learn about crystals and experience their positive energy.

Hide a select number of crystals around the house or yard and get the children to go on a treasure hunt to find them. You may set a time limit for an extra challenge. Make a list of the crystals you have hidden and a brief description of what each is known for or a fun fact about it or where it came from, so it is educational and enlightening as well as fun. When they find a crystal, have them figure out which one it is, tick it off the list, and go back to search for another one. This can be great for children's birthday parties too.

3. Crystal Fairy Garden

Another fun and creative activity for kids is to make a crystal fairy garden. This requires purchasing some fairy statues and/or ornaments for an outdoor garden, a potted minigarden, or an indoor makeshift garden. Collect a few fairies and other items like fairy furniture, fairy doors or gates, lamps, and stepping stones, and set them up in your garden setting with a selection of crystals. Search online for "fairy gardens," and you will find beautiful ideas. Turn your garden into a magical fairyland to delight your children and have them contribute too. You can even have a fairy mailbox and leave little notes for them to collect each week.

Children can add the crystals of their choice to the garden or allocate one crystal for each fairy. They might even like to name the fairy after the crystal. For example, Rosie for rose quartz and Amy for amethyst.

Just be sure to use crystals suitable for outdoor use, which is most crystals. Selenite can dissolve when wet, and others that are fragile or chip off easily are raw lepidolite and kyanite.

You also can make fairy ornaments or furniture, such as chairs or benches out of popsicle sticks, miniclotheslines out of two sticks and string, fairy clothing hanging from minipegs, and stepping stones made out of smooth flat rocks or bottle caps covered in paint, waterproof paper, or fabric.

4. Obstacle Course

This is a physical activity that can be done by children, or you can make a miniature variation of it using their toys.

Create an obstacle course at home or in a park with a few items. Have things to jump over, crawl under, or do something with, or an exercise such as jumping jacks, in order to move to the next obstacle and to the finish line. On the way, place crystals between the obstacles so that for each one they overcome, they get to take the crystal, place it down somewhere, and then go on to the next obstacle and the next crystal, until the course is completed. You can even have them identify each crystal from a list with photos. This is a good activity for kids' parties.

For the activity with their toys, help them create a miniobstacle course made out of various objects or exercises, with a crystal between each one. As they move their toy, such as an action figure or animal character, around the obstacle course, they can collect crystals along the way. They could play with a friend and have two obstacle courses and two toys going through at the same time within a time limit.

Some ideas for the obstacles could be something the toy has to hop over, helping out another toy in need, jumping on the spot ten times, doing a somersault in the air, and tidying up, so they are learning other skills and positive traits along the way. When they collect each crystal, help them to identify what it is and its "superpower."

5. **Teach your children the crystal affirmations.**

14 CONFIDENCE AND COMMUNICATION

What Does Confidence Look and Feel Like?

Confidence is the state of feeling completely comfortable and prepared. Wouldn't it be great to feel confident all the time? By tuning in to your authentic self and true nature and knowing deeply that you are enough just as you are, you can always be confident to handle whatever comes your way, without fear of being judged or rejected. So what does confidence look like to you? When you think of the word *confidence*, what images come to mind? How does it feel? What other emotions are enhanced? The more you can associate yourself with these feelings, the easier it will be to harness confidence in your life.

The Importance of Effective Communication

Communication is one of life's common challenges. Apart from love, acceptance, understanding, and dedication, communication is one of the most important factors in relationships and in business and career. Without effective communication, misunderstandings arise, feelings get hurt, and relationships and businesses are torn apart. Good communication always starts with yourself. When you communicate well with yourself, you are better equipped to do it effectively with others. This does not necessarily mean talking to yourself, although there is nothing wrong with that. It

is about listening more than anything, and then acknowledging and responding. Learn to listen and respond to yourself, and you will naturally be attuned to doing that with others. And when you communicate well with others, they are going to be more receptive and communicative with you.

How Can Crystals Support My Confidence and Communication?

Crystals can help you feel more confident because they tune in to the oneness of all things, the connected nature of us all, and the feeling of being not separate or different but a part of everything and everyone. Crystals and their high vibration can calibrate your own vibration to one that fosters greater self-acceptance and self-confidence, trusting in yourself and your abilities, in your uniqueness, and in the universe to always support and provide you with what is for your highest good. True confidence comes from within, and crystals help you tune that vibration from deep inside and remind you of your amazing power and worthiness.

Which Crystals Are Good for Enhancing Confidence and Communication?

Any crystal that makes you feel good or more connected to your true self will give you a boost of confidence, so pay attention to what you are drawn to. Six crystals in particular that can help you embody more confidence in daily life and make sure others' and your communication is effective and pleasant are tiger's eye, blue lace agate, aqua aura quartz, carnelian, sodalite, and lapis lazuli.

TIGER'S EYE

This crystal has browny-orange, tigerlike stripes and banding and holds a powerful energy of the earth to help ground and stabilize, while lifting the spirit to new heights and levels of awareness. It protects against conflicts and accusations, keeping the user in a state of calm and stable energy to move through the day more easily. It helps with dedication to a task and getting things done with confidence and certainty. It is a practical stone, working to achieve physical results via spiritual support and giving confidence and courage to get through any task.

* Balancing and grounding
* Uplifts and builds confidence
* Dedication and consistency
* Protective and supportive

⊱ Affirmation for Tiger's Eye ⊰
"I am courageously taking positive action each day."

BLUE LACE AGATE

Blue lace agate is one of the prettiest crystals. As its name suggests, it has a lacelike appearance with layers of curvy banding. Its light-blue colors give off a calming and serene vibe, and the layers are like soothing ripples or waves of music that reach us on a soul level. This crystal helps to support our most important relationship—the one with ourselves. It allows us to go deep within, layer by layer, to reveal underlying patterns and emotional habits that we may have developed over time during difficult situations. These learned responses are stored within and packed on top of one another. And for those that are not serving our best interests, we can begin to release them gradually and peacefully, with the help of this gentle but powerful crystal, and unravel the layers of our emotional pain and sensitivity.

When we discover and deal with our own issues, we begin to open up to new ways of understanding, not only ourselves but also other people, thereby helping our relationships to thrive through our newfound understanding and confidence. Blue lace agate clarifies our identity as spiritual human beings so that we may be unafraid of our emotions and let go of the fear of being ourselves or being judged. These layers have built up over time as a protective mechanism, and with gradual and conscious awareness and release, we can shed those unnecessary layers of fear and become our true selves with assurance. This crystal opens honest communication via the throat chakra. It allows our thoughts and feelings to become clear words and our true selves to be heard and acknowledged, and it brings our soul's wisdom out into the open to shine bright.

- Calming and soothing
- Emotional truth and freedom
- Honest communication
- Soulful self-expression

To help you fully embrace the power of blue lace agate for confidence and communication, read this message as though it is coming from a treasured friend.

Dear Unique Soul,

It is time for you to shine. You have many one-of-a-kind gifts to express, and it is safe to bring them out to be seen. It is all right to be who you are and offer this fearlessly.

Do not be afraid of your emotional or spiritual journey. You are on the right path, and each layer of awareness and release you go through is moving you farther along your true journey. And the more you travel this way, the more you step into the power of who you truly are.

Let what has scarred you in the past be what has built up your strength and resilience. Your history is your foundation, but it is not your future. It is the learning point for what is next. You are ready to move beyond old patterns and fully embrace the beautiful and unique soul that you are. Speak up, express yourself, and live authentically with confidence.

I believe in you.

Blue Lace Agate

᭝ Affirmation for Blue Lace Agate ᭝
"I am safe and supported in expressing my soul's truth."

AQUA AURA QUARTZ

This light and bright aqua-blue-colored crystal is made from quartz bonded with gold. Therefore, it has properties of both and produces its own unique gifts. Aqua aura is a crystal for communication in the physical and spiritual realms. It resonates with the throat chakra, which clears and calms communication and self-expression, and it assists with receiving messages from spirit, strengthening intuitive and psychic connections. It is helpful for confidence because it activates your full potential and encourages you to show your true and powerful self. It gets you to express yourself clearly and calmly, with your own unique light that will inspire others.

⚬ Clear communication

⚬ Confidence in your true self

⚬ Soul expression

⚬ Psychic enhancement

☞ Affirmation for Aqua Aura Quartz ☜
"The light of my soul shines through with peace and joy."

CARNELIAN

Carnelian is a great all-rounder because of its cleansing effect on the environment and other crystals. It is an essential part of any crystal kit. It can vary in color, usually consisting of combinations of red, orange, brown, pink, and cream. Carnelian is an overall balancer of body and mind and of the environment. It embodies stability and trust that all is well and moving confidently in the flow of life. This crystal has an enthusiastic yet stabilizing energy that can help with motivation and creativity, taking action and bringing out your best self through clear communication and expression so that you can enjoy life. It cleanses negativity and stress and empowers you with clarity and consistency.

- ❀ Powerful cleanser
- ❀ Enthusiasm and confidence for life
- ❀ Stability and trust
- ❀ Creativity and solutions

☙ Affirmation for Carnelian ❧
"I am confident in the clarity of my communication."

SODALITE

Sodalite is a blue-and-white-streaked crystal that is great for enhancing confidence and communication. It clears blockages and negative input from the environment so that thoughts can be clear and uncluttered, and it helps with group dynamics and interactions, aiding harmony and acceptance. Mentally, it encourages perception to be understanding and wise, and it allows individuals to speak with confidence and loving truth from a place of clear perspective. It unites all in a positive purpose, helping to keep the big picture relevant and front of mind so that you can avoid getting caught up in small issues that distract from a higher divine intent. Sodalite's benefit for confidence and communication excels when group or team communication is important.

- ❀ Clearing and calming
- ❀ Harmony and teamwork
- ❀ Understanding, acceptance, and truth
- ❀ Confident communication

꘎ Affirmation for Sodalite ꘎
*"My communication is loving and truthful,
and I express myself with confidence."*

LAPIS LAZULI

This rich royal-blue crystal with gold-colored flecks is an amazingly powerful stone for mental and spiritual wisdom, bringing clarity to any situation and the ability to express yourself truthfully and authentically. It helps you to tune in to universal intelligence and inspiration, stimulating creative thoughts, ideas, and solutions and boosting your intuition and psychic abilities. It also provides strength and connectedness to your environment so that you may integrate wisdom and truth into your life.

Lapis lazuli balances the throat chakra, which allows for assured communication and self-expression, confidence, and speaking the truth without fear. It lets you use your intuition to guide you and to live courageously as an authentic representation of your soul's truth.

- Wisdom and insight
- Inner power and confidence
- Communication and authentic expression
- Intuition and guidance

꘎ Affirmation for Lapis Lazuli ꘎
*"I am tuned into the unlimited
power of the universe."*

How Can I Use These Crystals for My Confidence and Communication?

Wear any of the blue-colored crystals (lapis lazuli, blue lace agate, aqua aura, or sodalite) as a short necklace so that it resonates with the throat chakra for truthful communication and expression.

Carry a tiger's eye crystal with you in your pocket or purse to any situations that require a boost of courage and confidence, such as job interviews, meetings, presentations, and social functions.

When communicating within a group, use sodalite to assist you with harmony and truth.

To clear your energy after challenging communications, **run a carnelian crystal over your body** in a sweeping movement. You can do this with selenite or black tourmaline too.

When communication involves using your intuition and speaking on the spot, without preparation, **have aqua aura quartz handy** for its assistance with connection to universal intelligence, awareness, and support.

Crystal Activities for Confidence and Communication

1. Throat Chakra Crystal Meditation
    Allow at least twenty minutes to lie down and focus on sending healing energy to your throat chakra. Place a light crystal such as blue lace agate, sodalite, aqua aura quartz, lapis lazuli, or blue calcite on your throat, and make sure

it is comfortable and will not fall off. You can rest an eye pillow on top of it if you need to hold it steady. Take three deep breaths, releasing built-up tension, and then breathe normally, relaxing your muscles more and more with each exhalation. Bring your attention to your throat area, feeling the oxygen passing through it and into your lungs. Let your awareness settle on the throat, visualizing a soft glowing ball of iridescent blue energy. Feel it nourishing all the physical structures in your throat and the cells vibrating with healthy, happy energy. See this energy sending out small radiations of light through your throat chakra and into the world around you, allowing your true nature to shine and your authentic self to be expressed with ease and confidence. Be at ease, knowing your throat chakra is clean and clear and vibrating at a frequency that allows your communication to be effective, honest, and caring.

Open your eyes when ready, and with an exhalation, release a sound like "ahhh," letting the energy connect with your voice box and activating it to help guide your words for the day ahead.

2. Try Something New

For a boost of confidence, choose a new activity or experience to try. Hold a tiger's eye crystal and a piece of aqua aura, and ask your inner self, "What is something I would like to experience but have not yet?" It could be a bucket list item, or it could be something quite simple like a new food, a new style of clothing, or going to a new yoga or meditation class. What makes you feel excited, joyful, and maybe even a little nervous? Try to step just outside your comfort zone (but not too much!) so that you are trying something you want to do but are not used to. Your confidence will get a workout, and afterward, it will be at a new higher level because you have done something out of the ordinary, which stimulates different areas of the brain and shows that you can experience new activities with confidence.

Depending on the activity, take a tiger's eye crystal with you or wear one as jewelry.

3. Crystallize Your Confidence and Communication

Think ahead to any events, meetings, or social occasions you have coming up in the next few weeks. How do you feel about each of them? For any that feel like they may take a bit of extra confidence or savvy communication skills, prepare crystals to use before, during, and after. Cleanse the crystals in moonlight or sunlight, and program them all together with the intention to enhance your confidence and communication. You also may like to program each one with a unique and specific purpose, such as sodalite to help you get through a challenging family conversation with ease and harmony, or tiger's eye to give you courage for an upcoming job interview, or blue lace agate to help you have a truthful personal discussion with someone close to you.

4. Communicate with Yourself

Schedule a regular chat with yourself. Get your favorite healthy beverage, light a candle, and have one or two crystals with you, such as carnelian and blue lace agate. You can add a rose quartz or rhodochrosite for self-love. Sit quietly for a moment and listen. Be aware of how you are feeling in your body and in your mind and in your heart. Acknowledge any positive or negative feelings, without judgment. Ask yourself any or all of the following questions, while holding one of your crystals.

How do I feel right now?

Is there anything I would rather be feeling right now?

What am I happy about in my life?

What am I unhappy or unsatisfied with in my life?

If I could do anything right now, what would it be?

Who do I enjoy talking to most in my life?

Does any part of my body need extra support right now? Is there anything I can do to nourish this area today?

What do I love about myself?

What is one of my best talents?

What does my soul want to say to me today? (Listen deeply and write down your answer, allowing words to flow naturally.)

You may wish to keep a self-communication journal
and ask these questions periodically. Remember: good
communication with the self is the foundation of all other
communication.

5. Complementary Tools and Tips to Use alongside Crystals

☀ Confident Clothing
What you choose to wear can have a strong effect
on your self-confidence and communication. Select
something with a style and color that reflects you, that
lifts your energy and makes you feel like you can handle
anything. Try a new color, maybe a bright-red or an
ocean-blue or a happy-yellow.

☀ Good Night's Sleep
This is important for your life, but particularly when you
have to communicate effectively or deal with a situation
confidently. We feel so much stronger and more assured
after a good night's rest, so make sure that you take steps
to optimize your sleep. Have a look at chapter 11, "Sleep
and Dreams," for some tips.

☀ Write It Down
If you want to be sure you communicate something
effectively, write it down first, either to have with you
to refer to or to get it off your mind, so you are clear on
what it is you want to say. If you are making a phone
call, note the main things you want to discuss and the
outcome you are aiming for, so you know when to

complete the conversation because the objective has been achieved or you have made progress.

☀ Aromatherapy Roll-Ons
Use a roller bottle to apply essential oils to your pulse points before any important events or when good communication is needed. Try clary sage, rosemary, peppermint, lemon, or orange.

6. Repeat the affirmations listed for each crystal when you need a confidence or communication boost, whether you have the crystal or not.

15 SPIRITUAL AND INTUITIVE DEVELOPMENT

About Spirituality

Spirituality is the awareness of the oneness of all things. It is the belief in a divine source of energy and love that is the foundation of all things and in this life force being everlasting and part of the universe as a whole. Being spiritual is remembering the spirit in all of us or SPIRIT-U-ALL (the spirit in you and in all).

What Is Intuition?

Intuition is the inner wisdom that comes to us and through us. It is a soft, pure, powerful nudging from our intelligent source, guiding and protecting us through daily life. Some call it a "gut instinct," a "sixth sense," or a "divine knowing." We all have access to intuition, and the more we utilize it, the stronger it gets and the more it is available to guide us in life.

For some, this intuitive power can be enhanced and cross into the next level (psychic awareness), where not only are intuitive nudges experienced, but also specific insights, visions, and knowings are discovered for the benefit of ourselves and other people.

How Can Crystals Help Develop My Intuition and Spiritual Connection?

Crystals can help with both intuition and psychic insight, as well as overall spiritual connection. Intuition and psychic ability happen at a level of high vibration and attunement to universal intelligence and awareness. Some people find it easy to tap into this, and for others it comes sporadically or the connection is there but not that strong.

Crystals, with their high-vibration energy, can help your own vibration match their frequency, raising your ability to tune in and connect more vividly. Some crystals are known for their greater connection to the spiritual and angelic realms, such as celestite, labradorite, and apophyllite, and can therefore enhance communication from one realm to another.

Crystals are a valuable accompaniment to a spiritual practice and to receiving intuitive or psychic insight and guidance, because they help focus your awareness and your questions and act as a conduit for receiving vibrations, which translate into thoughts or visions that bring information from the spiritual realm to the physical realm.

Which Crystals Are Good for Enhancing Spiritual and Intuitive Development?

To enhance your spiritual practice or intuitive ability, use amethyst, aqua aura quartz, lapis lazuli, labradorite, celestite, and apophyllite. To ground and protect yourself from negative energy or being overloaded with information from other people (during readings or in crowds, for example), use onyx, black tourmaline, and hematite.

AMETHYST

One of the most popular and well-known crystals is amethyst, which is recognized by its natural purple color. Widely available and often worn as jewelry, amethyst is often used with the body as tumbled stones and points or clusters and geodes for display. Some geodes are huge and give off an amazing energy. This is the crystal of intuition, calm and balance, clarity, and linking the physical to the spiritual. It is helpful in cases of illness, assisting with overall balancing of the body systems and emotional state. It calms overthinking, connects you with your source, and helps with overnight healing processes, so it is particularly useful for health conditions that are impacting on sleep. It can be very effective in enhancing meditation, particularly as part of a presleep ritual or a spiritual practice. Amethyst tunes you into your divine source and the healing power of the universe.

- Intuition and insight
- Calming and peaceful
- Overall balancing effect
- Transmits positive high vibrations to surroundings

⮞ **Affirmation for Amethyst** ⮜
*"I am connected at all times to
my powerful source energy."*

AQUA AURA QUARTZ

This light and bright aqua-blue-colored crystal is made from quartz bonded with gold. Therefore, it has properties of both and produces its own unique gifts. Aqua aura is a crystal for communication in the physical and spiritual realms. It resonates with the throat chakra, which clears and calms communication and self-expression, and it assists with receiving messages from spirit, strengthening intuitive and psychic connections. It is helpful for confidence because it activates your full potential and encourages you to show your true and powerful self. It gets you to express yourself clearly and calmly, with your own unique light that will inspire others.

- ☀ Clear communication
- ☀ Confidence in your true self
- ☀ Soul expression
- ☀ Psychic enhancement

☙ **Affirmation for Aqua Aura Quartz** ❧
"I am deeply connected to my soul and my spiritual gifts."

LAPIS LAZULI

This rich royal-blue crystal with gold-colored flecks is an amazingly powerful stone for mental and spiritual wisdom, bringing clarity to any situation and the ability to express yourself truthfully and authentically. It helps you to tune in to universal intelligence and inspiration, stimulating creative thoughts, ideas, and solutions and boosting your intuition and psychic abilities. It also provides strength and connectedness to your environment so that you may integrate wisdom and truth into your life.

Lapis lazuli balances the throat chakra, which allows for assured communication, speaking the truth, and expressing yourself without fear. It lets you use your intuition to guide you and to live courageously as an authentic representation of your soul's truth.

- Wisdom and insight
- Inner power and confidence
- Communication and authentic expression
- Intuition and guidance

ॐ **Affirmation for Lapis Lazuli** ॐ
"I am tuned into the unlimited power of the universe."

LABRADORITE

One of nature's most interesting crystals is labradorite. It has a shiny, bluish-purple iridescence against a dark-grayish background, with some areas of lighter creamy-yellow. It illuminates the inner power we all have, even if we cannot always see it, and brings to light our gifts and how we can share them with others. It is protective of psychic energy and enhances psychic insight and awareness into all realms and timelines. Labradorite embodies personal strength and trust in a higher power, as well as in the self and your intuition. It is a positive enhancer of all spiritual practices.

- Illuminating of gifts
- Psychic enhancement
- Strength and trust in the universe
- Protective

ॐ **Affirmation for Labradorite** ॐ
"I shine brightly with the light of the universe."

CELESTITE

Celestite is a pale-blue, icy-looking crystal with clusters that channels divine inspiration and intuitive creativity for artistic pursuits and problem-solving. It is a stone for boosting clairvoyance and angelic communication, and it can help with envisioning and imagination and bring this awareness into your present reality. Its pure, subtle vibrations lift your energy in an easy way, helping you bring this light into your life. It eases conflict resolution and keeps peace alive in all relationships, including the one with yourself, by dampening intense emotions and settling the mind and heart.

* Divine inspiration
* Creative and artistic ideas
* Visions and imagination
* Resolves conflict and problems

෨ **Affirmation for Celestite** ෬
*"I can create anything I want and
overcome all challenges."*

APOPHYLLITE

This beautiful clear and white clustered crystal often looks like quartz, but it has a whiter appearance and sometimes flecks of muted yellow or green colors. It is a great crystal for connecting your physical body with the spiritual realm, helping you to integrate insight and information into the present reality. It can bring forth past discoveries to shed light on the present and old emotional patterns that have been repressed and need to be released, allowing them to dissolve and disappear. It evokes calm and peace, helping you to focus on what is ahead and gaining insight to assist you on your spiritual journey.

* Spiritual connection and psychic insight
* Maintaining presence in the physical
* Releasing emotions
* Calming and settling

꙳ Affirmation for Apophyllite ꙴ
*"I am strongly connected to my physical self
and my spiritual self."*

ONYX

Onyx is a black stone, sometimes with a few small white or gray patches or bands. It is not as glassy in appearance compared to obsidian, which can help to distinguish the two. Onyx makes you feel strong and stable wherever you go, protecting you from sudden changes or negative influences in your surroundings, and can therefore be helpful for difficult or stressful situations. It is also beneficial for those who are sensitive and need to feel comfortable and safe in themselves. It assists with endurance and getting through challenges and long days, while creating a balance of energies around you. Spiritually, onyx can tune you into the past, helping you see what has happened and understand why, while also projecting into the future and allowing you access to what is on its way so that you can anticipate or adjust course. It is a useful stone for psychic readings and crystal communication.

* Protection and security
* Strength and endurance
* Spiritual awareness of past and future
* Balancing and stabilizing

ॐ Affirmation for Onyx ॐ
*"I am comfortable with my abilities and
protected from negative energy."*

BLACK TOURMALINE

Black tourmaline is a crystal that protects against radiation from electronic devices, as well as negative emotional energy. It transforms energy, absorbing that which is not beneficial and reforming it into a vibration that is more healthful. Because of its absorption ability, it benefits from regular cleansing so that it works more effectively. It also shields you from negative influences and can ease any disharmony that may be present. Tourmaline is like a guardian, creating a protective shield to maintain positive energy, especially when doing spiritual work, so that outside negative energies do not build up within you.

- Energy transformation
- Protector and guardian
- Provides a safe space for growth and nourishment
- Removes obstacles and blockages to well-being and intuition

> ❧ Affirmation for Black Tourmaline ☙
> *"My positive energy is protected and restored."*

HEMATITE

This silvery-gray, shiny crystal is a powerful stone of grounding, strength, power, and protection. It has an energetic vibration that encourages action and self-belief and clears negative energies from your energy field. It makes you aware of your personal habits and philosophies, giving you the wherewithal to choose and change your way of life to one that is for your highest good. It assists you on your life journey, providing energy and enthusiasm, and it helps you retain lessons along the way, building strength, resilience, and stamina. Hematite can both protect your energy and give you energy, and is best used in combination with other crystals that have a balancing effect and allow for a calm return to your center and core self.

- ⚜ Grounding
- ⚜ Protecting and guiding
- ⚜ Energy enhancer
- ⚜ Power and strength

ᘒ Affirmation for Hematite ᘔ
"My energy is strong and divinely protected."

How Can I Use These Crystals for My Spiritual and Intuitive Development?

Practice meditating with an amethyst, which is good for overall spiritual connection and intuition. Hold it in your hand or place it in between your eyebrows.

Wear a hematite ring to ground and protect your energy from psychic overload or negative input.

Keep an apophyllite cluster next to you while journaling or channeling insights, or hold it in your hands and close your eyes to ask for wisdom.

Try using two aqua aura quartz pieces, one in each hand, to tune in to your spirit guides and ask if they have any messages for you. If you have not yet experienced the presence of them, try the activity listed below to connect with them.

Create an altar or a space where you can display your favorite spiritual items, such as crystals, candles, sage sticks, incense, and statues. Regularly attune yourself to its energy by holding your palms out near it to absorb the positive energy, breathing it in and taking it with you. Occasionally pick up a crystal and ask, "What is in my best and highest good to know today?" This will help you get used to gaining wisdom and insight from your spiritual guides and your intuitive abilities.

If you get overwhelmed in crowds, take some black tourmaline or black onyx with you and allow it to filter out other people's negative energy so that it does not have to come directly through you.

Crystal Activities for Spiritual and Intuitive Development

1. **Connect with Your Spirit Guides**

   Everyone has one or more spiritual guides who are there to assist when asked. They may be those who have lived a human life or those who are purely spiritual in form. Some spirit guides are permanent; others are temporary and are there to help with specific phases or situations in life. The most important thing to know is these spiritual guides are always there for you, waiting for you to connect with them and ask for assistance. Whenever you do, they will hear and respond. Your requests are always being sorted out in the best way possible for the highest good of yourself and all involved, so trust them and trust your journey—the good and the bad—and know that you are being led on the path that is right for you.

You do not have to necessarily "meet" them or know their names, but it helps to have a personal connection and learn to recognize their signs.

You can say something like "Dear Guides, please help me with this situation so that it may go smoothly and have a positive outcome." Or "Dear Guides, I am feeling sad and would like you to help me with raising my vibration and being able to feel happy again."

To connect more directly with your spiritual guides, try the following exercise:

Write on a piece of paper: *"Dear Guides, I am now ready to connect with you, and I would love to ask if you could make yourself known to me during meditation, so I may cocreate with you to live a life aligned with my highest good."* Sign it with your name.

Place this paper underneath a pillow, keep a notepad or paper and pen handy, and lie down.

You may wish to play some relaxing music, light a candle, or do anything else you need to feel relaxed and tuned in. And, of course, have a crystal with you. Aqua aura or amethyst is good. Simply hold it in your hand, or place some on your heart area or on your third eye.

Take some slow breaths, and focus on each main part of your body, one by one, consciously relaxing the muscles and imagining a soft, gentle energy washing through the areas.

Now go deep within, imagining there is a core ball inside you that is 100 percent concentrated with source energy and love, which created you. It is gently pulsing and radiating, while remaining concentrated and focused within your being. Feel the love and the connection and the peace within yourself. Imagine yourself standing within this ball of energy, immersed in the wonderful feeling. Now, ask for one of your spirit guides to come forward. See a figure moving toward you as though through a mist, into this ball of energy, to meet you where you are. Do not judge what you see or try to create a person's appearance. Just see what you see, even if it is not clear. You may recognize a figure that is very detailed and looks like a real person or you may notice a silhouette and shapes more than features. You may see colors or feel a certain sensation, like warmth or a fresh breeze, or smell a certain flower. Let your spirit guide come to you in any way, shape, or form. Smile at them, and say thank you. Ask them what their name is. If nothing comes, do not worry. Just be aware of any name that comes to mind first. Ask what they are here to help you with, and listen for a reply. You may hear their words not by sound, but by awareness and knowing. Listen from the soul. They may be here to teach you, helping you learn lessons in life. Or they may say they are here for a more specific reason, such as to help you get through a health challenge or a relationship problem. Thank them for being there, embrace them, and either end your meditation session or ask for them to bring the next spirit guide through.

You might find it best to meet only three or four at first, and these may be all that come through. Or you may meet more in future sessions. When you end your meditation, write down their names, if any came to you, and what they are there to help you with. When communicating with your spiritual guides from now on, you can refer to them in general as guides or you can call on a specific guide by name.

2. Writing from the Soul

Get a sheet of paper and choose a crystal to channel insight from your soul and spirit. An apophyllite cluster placed on a desk or on the top part of your paper or in your hand is good. Aqua aura, amethyst, and labradorite are also fine choices. Take a few moments to quiet your mind and focus on yourself as a spiritual being. Holding the crystal and a pen, say, "I ask that any information that is for my highest good right now be transmitted through this pen and on to the page. Thank you." Now write whatever your pen wants to write. You can start with a question, or let it be about anything. It may come out as fully formed beautiful sentences, or it may be key words and random phrases, song lyrics, anything. Do not judge. Do not let the brain kick in. Just let the pen move across the page, acting as your soul's scribe. If you have asked a question, such as "Should I let go of this friendship?" or "What will help me most in my relationship right now?" your writing may appear to be by someone else, addressed to you, or it may come out as "I" this and "I" that, as though you are advising yourself. Emotions may come up, and this is a good thing. It is energy moving through you, being released and heard. When you feel you have written enough or have a clear answer, thank your soul and spirit and the crystal for its assistance. Read over what you have written and see if it makes sense to you. You might just find you have been given some of the best advice you have received. I did this for a difficult issue I was facing, and I got clear answers and "permission" to do what I was worried about doing but deep down wanted to do. The writing exposed the reasons behind the challenges and what the outcome of my decision would be. It helped me move forward, and it is a technique I will continue to use because sometimes listening to our own spirit is the best guidance.

3. Oracle Card Readings

Oracle cards and crystals are fantastic companions when doing spiritual work. Card decks, for me, have been almost like crystals; I can never have too many! I love the artwork and inspiring messages on them and seeing what guidance they have for me at any given time. They are usually spot-on. When they are combined with crystals, I find the insight even more accurate and relevant. The crystals go deeper into the question or issue, to better interpret and understand the answer.

Oracle cards are different from tarot cards, but they can give a similar understanding of a situation, just in different ways. Tarot is a more specific method of card reading, with recurring types of cards and symbolism, and can require more training to understand. Oracle cards usually have specific insights written on them and the meaning is easily understood by simply reading the cards or the descriptions in an accompanying booklet.

With oracle cards, you can do a simple one-card reading or multiple-card readings and layouts for deeper insight.

Just picking one card from a deck can give you an answer to a question, insight into an issue, or simply some "random" guidance.

If you have a new card deck, it works best if you activate it first. There are various ways to do this, and some decks will have specific instructions on them, in which case follow the guidelines. Otherwise, cleanse the deck with some burning sage or sage spray if it is a second-hand one, or has been touched by many people while in a store. Use a black stone like tourmaline or onyx to rub over the card deck and absorb any remaining energy or a carnelian as a general cleanser. You also can keep a carnelian on top of your card deck when not in use to keep it clean. Open the deck, and tap it three times with your knuckles. Then blow on it to disperse the energy. You can rub a new crystal over it, such as aqua aura or amethyst, to enhance spiritual connection. Now, hold the deck to your heart and ask for it to be helpful and accurate for yourself and others. Next, pick up each card one at a time and say, "Thank you for your accurate insight" and then place it down. Keep doing this with the whole deck until all the cards have been touched and thanked. Then place the cards in their box. It may seem tedious, but once it is done, it is done, and your deck will work really well at showing the most relevant answers.

When you are ready to do a reading, start with yourself. Hold the cards to your heart and ask a question or ask to receive the most relevant guidance to help you right now. Shuffle the cards, and stop when you feel like it. If a number pops into your head, like four, take the fourth card from the top. Read the card, and take note of its insight and how it may relate to your situation. Thank the card, place it back, and draw another one. When placing your card back in the deck, it is helpful to tap it and blow the energy away, so it is fresh for the next reading.

If you would like more overall insight, do a three-card reading, with the first card being more relevant to the past, the second to the present, and the third to the future.

4. Crystal-Clear Answers

Ask a crystal a question. You may feel a bit silly at first, but do not worry. Remember, it is a conduit for spiritual wisdom and for your own intuition. It is simply using its stored knowledge from millions of years of existence, along with present-day awareness and your thoughts, to transmit a relevant and helpful response via energy, which you will receive via thought.

Take a crystal, ask it to be of assistance with a question you have, and then ask the question. Hold the crystal and close your eyes, breathing slowly, and allow any answers or thoughts to come. Let them solidify and become coherent, and open your eyes when you feel the transmission is complete. Alternatively, you can leave your eyes open and write down your answers as they come.

Thank the crystal for its help and act on its guidance.

5. Spiritual Connection Circle (or New Moon Circle)

This is a beautiful activity to do when you have more time available or want to create a special ceremony or ritual.

You also can do this with a group of people for even greater benefit or make it a regular monthly gathering.

On the floor or outside on the ground, weather permitting, create a spiritual crystal circle. This is like a giant crystal grid that you sit next to and perform an intention or gratitude ceremony or that each person sits around in a circle.

You might like to play music, burn incense or a candle, or diffuse essential oils while preparing the circle. Use a round flat plate, an old clock, a cake stand, or a special crystal grid and sacred geometry base, and place it down to begin. Select your crystals based on your intention or purpose for the ceremony. For a general spiritual connection circle, use a quartz point or smoky quartz or amethyst in the center. Surround the center point with small stones, such as blue lace agate or sodalite, for communication, especially if doing the circle as part of a group. Use the same number of communication crystals as there are people. For the radiating spokes, use aqua aura shards and/or amethyst. You also can add red jasper to ground your energy and bring in the earth element to harmonize with the spiritual realm. Around the outer circle, add a few stones of lapis lazuli or labradorite or extra amethyst, and intersperse these with small crystal chips of your choice, such as amazonite for harmony and protection from negative energy or rose quartz to enhance loving connection. This crystal grid will form the energy center of the circle.

Around the center, add a circle of flower petals and leaves and a few tea-light candles. Make sure they are not too close to the petals and leaves. Now create spokes radiating out, using twigs, small branches, or flowers with long stems. Between these, add smaller branches or flowers and feathers, if you have any. If you are in a group, have everyone add pieces to the circle.

When it is complete, light the candles and start your ceremony. You may like to open with a prayer or intention and then some minutes of quiet reflection, looking at the circle, focusing on your breathing, singing or chanting, or journaling. If it is a spiritual connection or insight circle, each person may ask a question out loud or silently. Then, through quiet reflection and journaling, they write the answers they receive and share with the group afterward. You also can have each person say something they wish to release and something they wish to bring into their life, while holding a crystal and passing it around. This way you are harnessing the power not only of crystals but of group intention, enhancing the spiritual energy of the intentions. End with a gratitude prayer or statement and any other positive contributions, and blow out the candles. Your circle is complete, and you can either begin dismantling it with reverence or keep it where it is.

Holding a regular circle gathering and ceremony is a great way to maintain a strong spiritual connection, enhance manifestations, and strengthen relationship bonds. It can be done at any time: on a full moon or new moon or to recognize specific milestones or events in life, such as birthdays, anniversaries, a new home, or the start of a new season.

I hope you enjoy the many creative and inspiring ways to use crystals in your life. May they enhance your well-being in mind, body, and spirit.

ACKNOWLEDGMENTS

I would like to say thank you to my agent, Joelle Delbourgo, for asking me if I was interested in writing a book about crystals, which set the ball rolling, culminating in this book. Thanks also for your help in securing a publishing contract, and thanks to Jennifer Feldman, publisher, Fiona Hallowell, acquisitions editor, and Ixia Press/Dover Publications for choosing to publish this book. I am incredibly grateful it has found a home with you! Thanks also are due to the design team, John M. Alves and Alexis Capitini, for the eye-catching cover and the layout, and to the editing team, Stephanie Castillo Samoy and Sally Fay, for their careful and precise work to help this book become the best it could be.

I would like to thank Belinda Doyle at Belinda Doyle Design for the beautiful photography featured and Natasha Cuevas at Tashi for her creative vision and styling for the photo shoot, as well as for being the person to suggest I "start a little crystal shop." Somehow, everything snowballed from there! Thank you to Hot Mess Body for the bath products, to Willow Flower Bar for the flowers, and to Judy Hall for *The Crystal Bible.*

Thanks to Emily, Natasha, Sheree, and staff at the Collective Beat and Chatterbox Market for helping me make my crystal passion a reality through my store, Hart and Soul Studio. And thanks to my customers and clients who purchase crystals and attend readings and workshops. I am grateful to be able to do what I love and share the joy of crystals with others.

To my parents, who always encourage and support me with every new venture I undertake, I thank you. And to my friends, who get excited with me when I release a new book and support me with friendly chats, company, understanding, and positivity, I thank you too.

Thanks to my son, Jayden, for being who you are and for carrying heavy boxes of crystals to the shop when needed!

And a big thank-you to my partner, Zeynel, for supporting me 100 percent with my crystal passion. You bring so much heart to Hart and Soul. Thank you for taking on a lot of the behind-the-scenes work: putting furniture together, building shop structures, making crystal digging kits, running workshops and activities with me, and sticking hundreds of price tags on to products! Not to mention encouraging my writing and always being there. You are a gem (pun intended).

And, last, I thank God for the many beautiful, powerful, and unique gifts provided in our earth, of which crystals are a special part.

INDEX OF CRYSTALS

An alphabetical list of the fifty crystals described in this book and the pages to find them on:

Agate, 7, 8, 19, 90, 92, 93, 94, 133, 190

Amazonite, 64, 65, 69, 94, 99, 100, 101, 106, 107, 112, 117, 120, 228

Amber, 31, 35, 36, 37, 39, 172, 173, 177

Amethyst, 7, 10, 15, 24, 25, 42, 83, 94, 138, 159, 161, 162, 165, 167, 172, 173, 191, 193, 212, 213, 220, 222, 224, 226, 228

Ametrine, 172, 173

Apophyllite, 172, 212, 217, 220, 224

Aqua aura quartz, 197, 200, 201, 204, 212, 213, 214, 220

Aquamarine, 90, 91, 92, 94, 112, 117, 118, 120, 185, 188, 189, 192

Aventurine (green), 21, 56, 58, 60, 61, 83, 120, 149, 150, 152, 154, 172

Black tourmaline, 1, 11, 37, 70, 83, 105, 106, 188, 204, 212, 218, 219, 221

Blue calcite, 172, 173, 174, 175, 204

Blue lace agate, 64, 66, 67, 68, 69, 71, 122, 197, 198, 199, 200, 204, 206, 207, 228

Carnelian, 11, 18, 70, 83, 138, 172, 197, 201, 202, 204, 207, 226

Celestite, 18, 27, 212, 216

Citrine, 7, 11, 21, 42, 46, 47, 49, 94, 120, 149, 152, 153, 154, 155, 172, 173

Dalmatian jasper, 185, 187, 188, 192

Emerald, 76, 81, 83

Fluorite, 15, 94, 112, 115, 116, 120

Garnet, 76, 79, 80, 128, 130, 134, 136, 137, 172

Hematite, 172, 212, 219, 220

Howlite (white), 35, 159, 160, 165, 191

Herkimer diamond, 159, 162, 163, 167

Jade, 31, 33, 34, 37, 39, 76, 81, 83, 149, 151, 154, 172, 190

Kyanite, 11, 13, 24, 185, 186, 192, 193

Labradorite, 25, 129, 212, 215, 224, 228

Lapis lazuli, 18, 172, 173, 174, 197, 203, 204, 212, 214, 215, 228

Larimar, 56, 58, 59, 60, 61

Lepidolite, 42, 44, 45, 49, 159, 160, 161, 165, 193

Mahogany obsidian, 112, 118, 119, 120, 121

Mookaite, 31, 33, 37, 39, 128, 131, 132, 134, 135, 141

Moonstone, 83, 128, 129, 134, 135, 136, 137, 138

Obsidian, 42, 48, 114, 187, 218

Onyx (black), 112, 114, 115, 119, 185, 187, 191, 212, 218, 221, 226

Peach selenite, 42, 43, 44, 49, 50

Peacock ore, 18, 185, 189

Peridot, 172, 173, 175, 176

Pink agate, 92, 128, 133, 135, 141

Pyrite, 112, 116, 117, 149, 150, 151, 152, 154

Quartz, 6, 11, 15, 19, 23, 25, 39, 42, 62, 94, 99, 102, 103, 106, 107, 154, 162, 172, 213, 217, 228

Red jasper, 42, 47, 48, 112, 113, 119, 172, 173, 177, 178, 228

Rhodochrosite, 51, 56, 59, 60, 61, 64, 68, 69, 71, 76, 78, 79, 85, 207

Rhodonite, 76, 79

Rose quartz, 8, 10, 21, 23, 24, 42, 45, 46, 49, 51, 56, 57, 58, 60, 61, 62, 71, 73, 76, 77, 78, 82, 85, 90, 93, 94, 107, 128, 129, 130, 134, 135, 136, 137, 138, 141, 154, 172, 193, 207, 228

Selenite, 11, 13, 24, 71, 83, 99, 100, 101, 105, 108, 128, 131, 134, 135, 179, 193, 204

Sodalite, 64, 65, 66, 69, 71, 73, 90, 91, 94, 95, 99, 103, 104, 106, 112, 113, 114, 119, 172, 197, 202, 203, 204, 228

Tiger's eye, 172, 185, 186, 190, 191, 197, 198, 204, 205, 206

Tourmaline, 24, 94, 99, 101, 102, 119, 138, 219, 226

Turquoise, 31, 34, 35, 37, 39, 160, 172

Unakite, 31, 32, 37, 39, 128, 132, 133, 135

Watermelon tourmaline, 76, 82, 83, 119

Yellow jasper, 172, 173, 176

ABOUT THE AUTHOR

Juliet Madison is a best-selling author of fiction and nonfiction, including romantic comedies such as the Amazon best seller *Fast Forward*, the romantic small-town Tarrin's Bay series, and the young adult supernatural series *The Delta Girls*. She has written and illustrated the inspirational coloring book for adults *Color Your Dreams* and is the author of the self-help journal *The Secret Letters Project*, which sparked the worldwide kindness initiative #secretlettersproject, encouraging people to write inspiring letters to strangers.

Juliet lives on the south coast of New South Wales, Australia, owns a crystal pop-up shop, teaches empowering workshops and courses, and does one-on-one intuitive crystal readings and spiritual coaching sessions.

You can share photos or experiences of how you incorporate crystals in your life in Juliet's Facebook group, The Power of Crystals, or tag her on social media (use the hashtag #thepowerofcrystalsbook). Connect with Juliet online via The Power of Crystals page at www.julietmadison.com, or on Facebook: @julietmadisonauthor, Instagram: @julietmadisonauthorartist, and Twitter: @juliet_madison.